US NAVAL VESSELS, 1943

US NAVAL VESSELS
1943

Introduction by A. D. Baker III

NAVAL INSTITUTE PRESS

Published and distributed in the United States of America
by the Naval Institute Press, Annapolis, Maryland 21402.

This edition is authorized for sale only in
the United States, its territories and possessions.

Originally published in 1943
as *ONI-54 Series U.S. Naval Vessels*
by the U.S. Division of Naval Intelligence

Library of Congress Catalog Card No
85-63349
ISBN 0-87021-724-0

Printed and bound in Great Britain by The Bath Press.

INTRODUCTION

As the official introduction by the then-Director of Naval Intelligence, Rear-Admiral R. E. Schuirmann, USN, indicates, the November 1943 issue of *U.S. Naval Vessels (ONI-54 Series)* represented a consolidation and updating of the U.S. Navy's principal ship recognition document for its own fleet. As a historical document, it is invaluable, as it presents a comprehensive portrait of the fleet at the period where it was beginning to expand into the vast armada that ultimately overwhelmed enemy forces at sea. In mid-war, the ships showed the advances in equipment and protection prompted by early combat experience, yet they still betrayed their pre-war elegance of design, having not yet had their symmetry destroyed by crowds of anti-aircraft gun and director tubs or by complex thickets of radar and countermeasures antennas.

The photography used in *ONI-54* was selected from a Naval Intelligence Division collection that at the time was approaching some 50,000 8-inch prints. The views incorporated were intended to enable the user to recognize as friendly the hundreds of classes of U.S. Navy ships from virtually any angle. Scaled and shaded line drawings were prepared (usually by trained architects, who found themselves at ONI drafting boards for the duration of the war) either from General Arrangement Booklet plans or from simplified, smaller-scale recognition plans done by the builder's yard or repair yards each time a ship was completed or altered. Data in *ONI-54* were kept to a minimum, and the text confined itself to pointing out salient recognition features or differences between units within a class.

The excellence of the photography and scrupulously accurate plans should make this book of value to historians, enthusiasts and model builders. The publishers have made every effort to reproduce as perfectly as possible the appearance of the original (aside from presenting it in a hard cover, rather than as a post-bound paperback) and have used an actual working copy, binder holes and all.

A. D. BAKER III

ONI 54 SERIES
U. S. NAVAL VESSELS

1. The O. N. I. 54 Series has passed through many transitions as a result of wartime conditions. First published as O. N. I. 54, Silhouettes of U. S. Naval Ships, the manual has since been issued as O. N. I. 54–R, U. S. Naval Ships and Aircraft, in the standard O. N. I. 6 x 10 size for use in U. S. Navy Task Binders. The continued appearance of new ships, and reconstruction of older vessels, necessitated the issue of this manual in a series of supplements. As data became available in increasing quantities, collation of the material has imposed a considerable burden upon the user.

2. The advanced status of the naval building program now makes it possible to reprint this publication in more convenient form and the greater part of the manual will henceforth be issued in a series of "type pamphlets" which will be issued as reconstruction and the completion of new ships require. The process of replacement of material already issued will necessarily be a gradual one. Material covering types will be reissued in pamphlet form as it becomes available and these pamphlets may be substituted by holders of O. N. I. 54–R for the loose-leaf sheets covering these types.

3. O. N. I. 54–R was initially issued under the title "U. S. Naval Ships and Aircraft." Since coverage on U. S. aircraft in standard 6 x 10 size is now available in other publications, an aircraft section will not be included in the O. N. I. 54 Series as reissued. The O. N. I. 54 Series illustrates all types of seagoing vessels on the Navy list.

R. E. SCHUIRMANN,
Rear Admiral, U. S. Navy,
Director of Naval Intelligence.

U.S. BATTLESHIPS

The appearance of U. S. Battleships, since the outbreak of the war, has evolved into a predominantly one-stack design. Although similar in general outline, these one-stackers may be differentiated by their armament dispositions and hull lines. Of the two stack BB's, COLORADO alone is likely to undergo radical alteration of appearance.

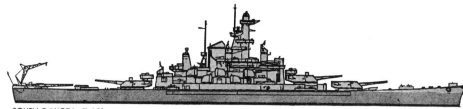

SOUTH DAKOTA CLASS

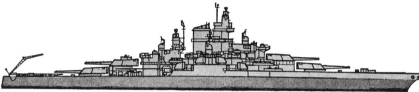

TENNESSEE CLASS

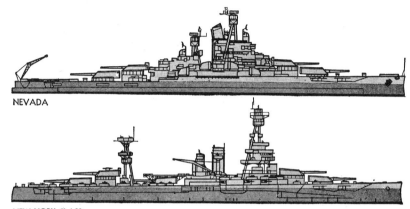

NEVADA

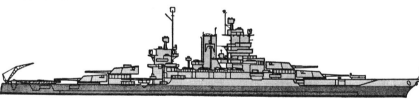

NEW MEXICO CLASS

NEW YORK CLASS

PENNSYLVANIA

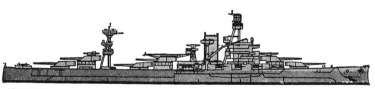

ARKANSAS

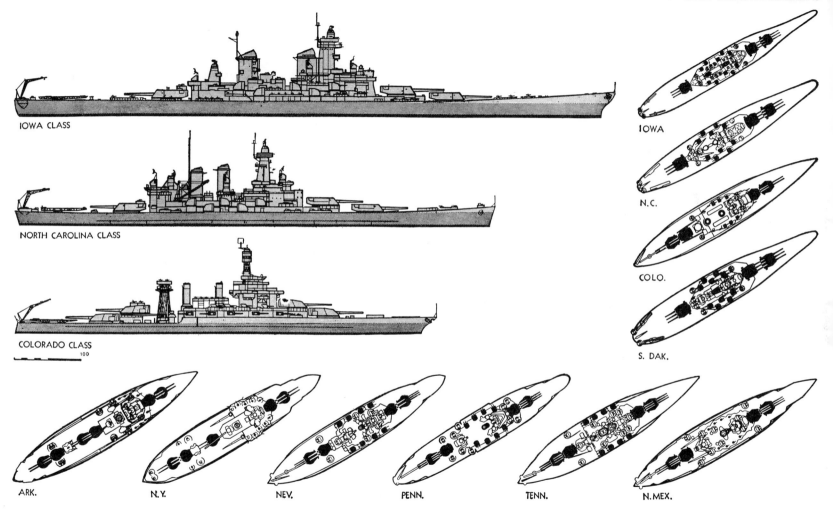

IOWA CLASS

NORTH CAROLINA CLASS

COLORADO CLASS

100

IOWA

N.C.

COLO.

S. DAK.

ARK.

N. Y.

NEV.

PENN.

TENN.

N. MEX.

U. S. CRUISERS

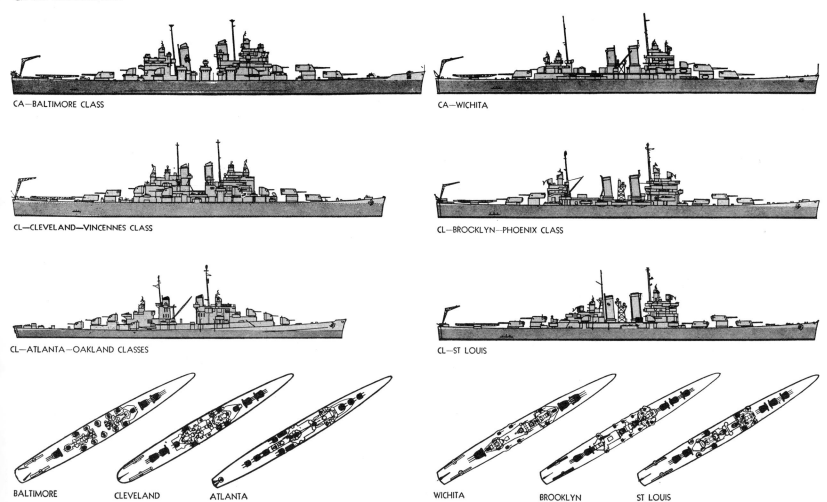

CA—BALTIMORE CLASS

CA—WICHITA

CL—CLEVELAND—VINCENNES CLASS

CL—BROCKLYN—PHOENIX CLASS

CL—ATLANTA—OAKLAND CLASSES

CL—ST LOUIS

BALTIMORE

CLEVELAND

ATLANTA

WICHITA

BROOKLYN

ST LOUIS

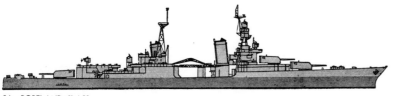

CA—PORTLAND CLASS

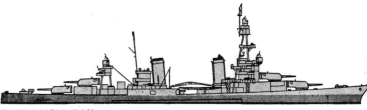

CA—NEW ORLEANS CLASS

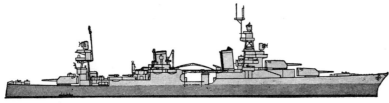

CA—AUGUSTA

CA—PENSACOLA CLASS

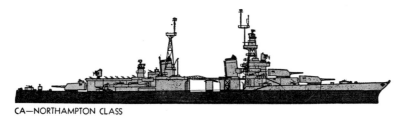

CA—NORTHAMPTON CLASS

100

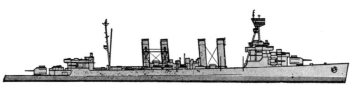

CL—OMAHA CLASS

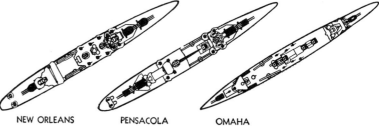

PORTLAND   AUGUSTA   NORTHAMPTON   NEW ORLEANS   PENSACOLA   OMAHA

U. S. CARRIERS

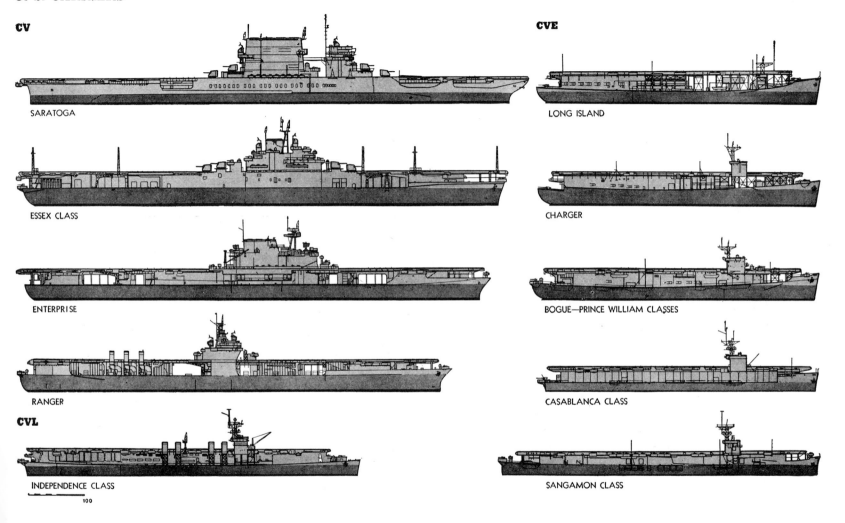

CV

SARATOGA

ESSEX CLASS

ENTERPRISE

RANGER

CVL

INDEPENDENCE CLASS

100

CVE

LONG ISLAND

CHARGER

BOGUE—PRINCE WILLIAM CLASSES

CASABLANCA CLASS

SANGAMON CLASS

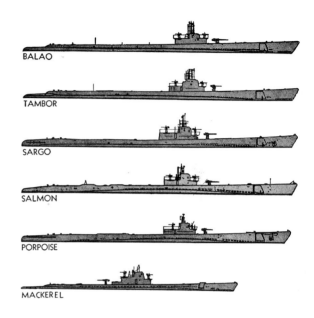

BALAO

TAMBOR

SARGO

SALMON

PORPOISE

MACKEREL

R CLASS

S CLASS

These photos and silhouettes are typical of the appearance changes completed in U. S. Submarines. Once distinctive, these ships now greatly resemble most Axis types, which may be found illustrated in the ONI 220 series.

NARWHAL

100

BASS

DESTROYERS

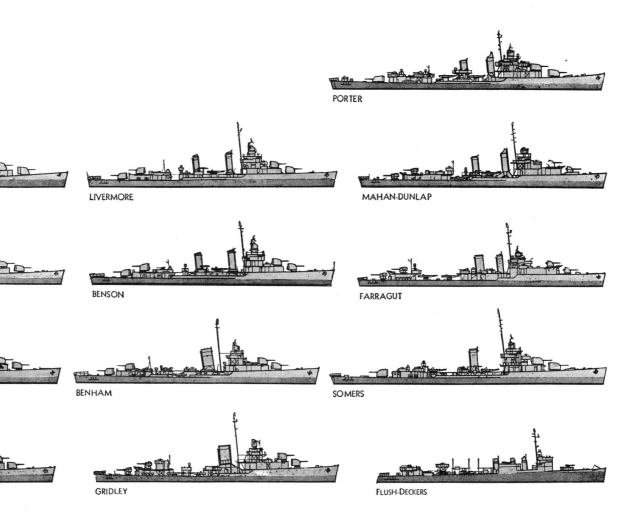

PORTER

SUMNER

LIVERMORE

MAHAN-DUNLAP

FLETCHER

BENSON

FARRAGUT

SIMS

BENHAM

SOMERS

BAGLEY

100

GRIDLEY

FLUSH-DECKERS

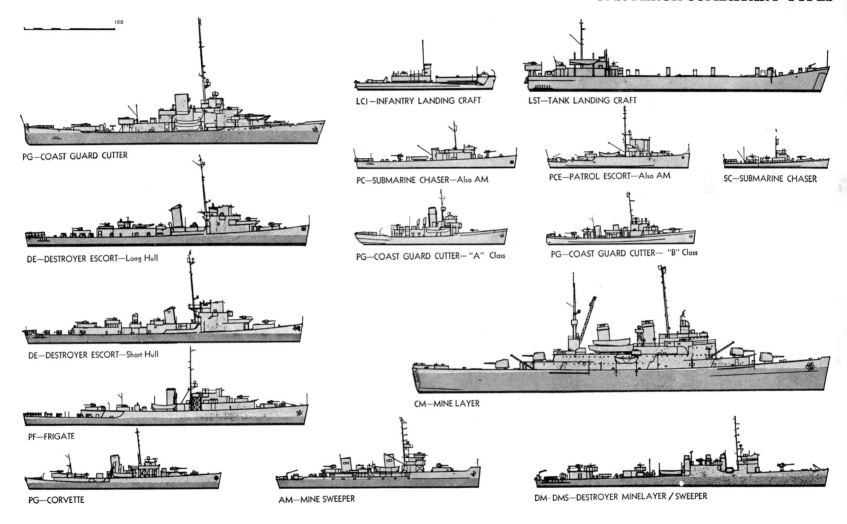

100

PG—COAST GUARD CUTTER

DE—DESTROYER ESCORT—Long Hull

DE—DESTROYER ESCORT—Short Hull

PF—FRIGATE

PG—CORVETTE

LCI—INFANTRY LANDING CRAFT

LST—TANK LANDING CRAFT

PC—SUBMARINE CHASER—Also AM

PCE—PATROL ESCORT—Also AM

SC—SUBMARINE CHASER

PG—COAST GUARD CUTTER— "A" Class

PG—COAST GUARD CUTTER— "B" Class

CM—MINE LAYER

AM—MINE SWEEPER

DM-DMS—DESTROYER MINELAYER / SWEEPER

U.S. NAVAL AUXILIARIES

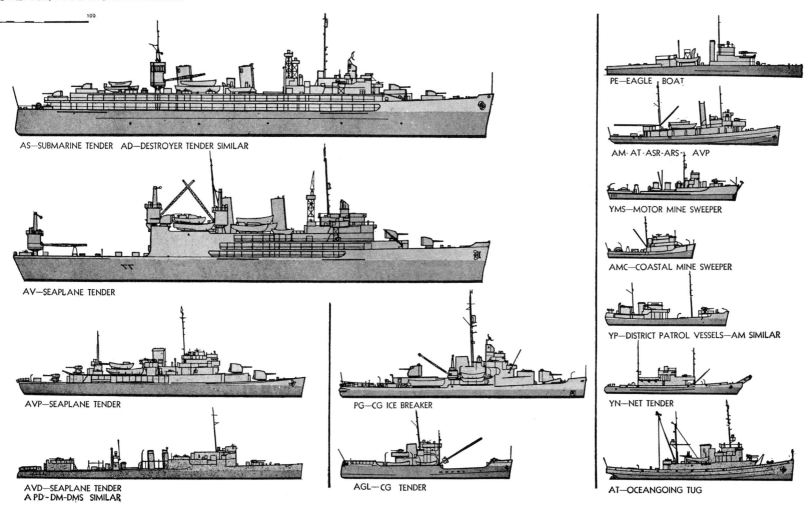

100

AS—SUBMARINE TENDER AD—DESTROYER TENDER SIMILAR

AV—SEAPLANE TENDER

AVP—SEAPLANE TENDER

AVD—SEAPLANE TENDER
A PD–DM–DMS SIMILAR

PG—CG ICE BREAKER

AGL—CG TENDER

PE—EAGLE BOAT

AM· AT·ASR·ARS· AVP

YMS—MOTOR MINE SWEEPER

AMC—COASTAL MINE SWEEPER

YP—DISTRICT PATROL VESSELS—AM SIMILAR

YN—NET TENDER

AT—OCEANGOING TUG

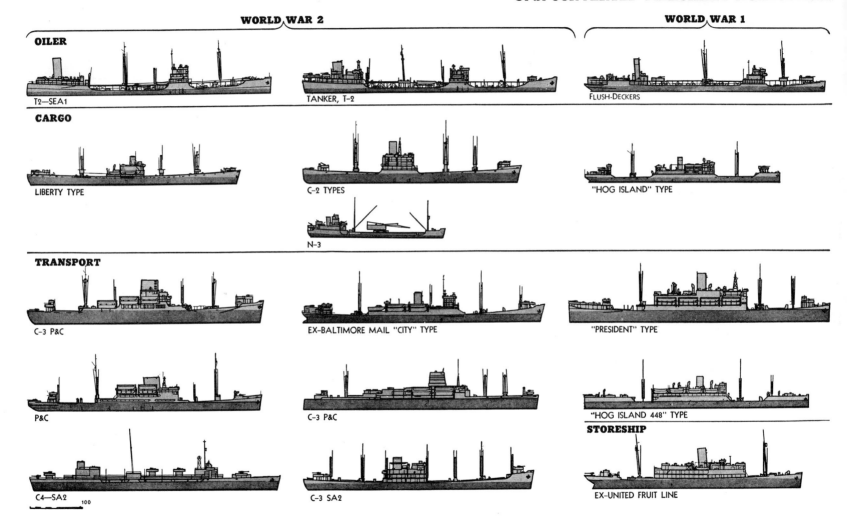

WORLD WAR 2 **WORLD WAR 1**

OILER

T2—SEA1   TANKER, T-2   FLUSH-DECKERS

CARGO

LIBERTY TYPE   C-2 TYPES   "HOG ISLAND" TYPE

N-3

TRANSPORT

C-3 P&C   EX-BALTIMORE MAIL "CITY" TYPE   "PRESIDENT" TYPE

P&C   C-3 P&C   "HOG ISLAND 448" TYPE

STORESHIP

C4—SA2   C-3 SA2   EX-UNITED FRUIT LINE

100

U. S. Naval Vessels—Type Designations

PRINCIPAL COMBATANT TYPES

BB —Battleship
CB —Large Cruiser
CV —Aircraft Carrier
CVB —Large Aircraft Carrier
CVL —Aircraft Carrier (light)
CVE —Aircraft Carrier (escort)
CA —Heavy Cruiser
CL —Light Cruiser
DD —Destroyer
DE —Destroyer Escort Vessel
SS —Submarine

MINOR COMBATANT TYPES

CM —Minelayer
DM —Light Minelayer
DMS —High-Speed Minesweeper
AM —Minesweeper
AMc —Coastal Minesweeper
AN —Net-laying Ship
PF —Frigate
PE —Eagle Boat
PG —Gunboat
PGM —Motor Gunboat
PC —Submarine Chaser
PCE —Patrol Craft Escort
PCER —Patrol Craft, Escort Rescue
PCS —Submarine Chaser (136')
SC —Submarine Chaser (110')
PT, —Motor Torpedo Boat
PTC —Motor Torpedo Boat
PY, PYc—Yacht

NAVAL AUXILIARIES

TENDERS

AD —Destroyer Tender
AH —Hospital Ships
AS —Submarine Tender
ASR —Submarine Rescue Vessel
AR —Repair Ship
ARB —Battle Damage Repair Ship

ARG —Internal Combustion Engine Repair Ship
ARH —Hull Repair Ships
ARL —Landing Craft Repair Ship
ARS —Salvage Vessel
AV —Seaplane Tender
AVD —Destroyer Seaplane Tender
AVP —Small Seaplane Tender
AGP —Motor Torpedo Boat Tender

CARGO AND FUEL SHIPS

AE —Ammunition Ships
AF —Provision Storeship
AK —Cargo Ship
AKA —Attack Cargo Ships
AKN —Net Cargo Ship
AKS —Stores Issue Ships
AKV —Cargo Ship & Aircraft Ferry
AO —Oiler
AOG —Gasoline Tanker

TRANSPORTS

AP —Troop Transport
APA —Attack Transport
APD —High-Speed Transport
APH —Wounded Evacuation Transport
APM —Mechanized Artillery Transport
APR —Rescue Transport
APS —Auxiliary Transport, Submarine
APV —Aircraft Transport
AGC —Combined Operations—Communications Headquarters Ship
SMT —Special Military Type

LANDING CRAFT

LCC —Landing Craft, Control
LCI —Landing Craft, Infantry
LCM —Landing Craft, Mechanized Equipment
LCP —Landing Craft, Personnel
LCP(N)—Landing Craft, Personnel (Nested)

LCP(R)—Landing Craft, Personnel (Ramp)
LCR —Landing Craft, Rubber
LCS —Landing Craft, Support
LCT —Landing Craft, Tank
LCV —Landing Craft, Vehicle
LCVP—Landing Craft, Vehicle-Personnel
LSD —Landing Ship, Dock
LSM —Landing Ship, Medium
LST —Landing Ship, Tank
LVT —Landing Vehicle, Tracked

BASE CRAFT

AB —Crane Ship
ABD —Advance Base Dock
ABSD—Advance Base Sectional Dock
AFD —Mobile Floating Dock
APL —Barracks Ship
APc —Coastal Transport
ARDC—Concrete Repair Dock
ARD —Floating Drydock
AT —Oceangoing Tug
ATR —Rescue Tug
AVC —Catapult Lighter
AVR —Aircraft Rescue Vessel
AMb —Harbor Minesweeper

MISCELLANEOUS

AG —Miscellaneous Auxiliaries
AGS —Surveying Ship
IX —Unclassified

DISTRICT CRAFT

YAG —Miscellaneous District Auxiliaries
YMS —Motor Minesweeper
YMT —Motor Tug
YN —Net Tender
YNg —Gate Tender
YNT —Tug Class Net Tender

YP —District Patrol Vessel
YT —Harbor Tug
CMc —Coastal Mine Layer

BARGES

YCD —Fueling Barge
YOG —Gasoline Barge
YO —Fuel-oil Barge
YOS —Oil Storage Barge
YPK —Pontoon Storage Barge
YS —Stevedoring Barge
YSR —Sludge Removal Barge
YTT —Torpedo Testing Barge
YW —Water Barge

LIGHTERS

YA —Ash Lighter
YC —Open Lighter
YCK —Open Cargo Lighter
YCV —Aircraft Transport Lighter
YF —Covered Lighter
YFT —Torpedo Transport Lighter
YG —Garbage Lighter
YLA —Open Landing Lighter

MISCELLANEOUS

YCF —Car Floats
YD —Floating Derrick
YDG —Degaussing Vessel
YDT —Diving Tender
YE —Ammunition Tender
YFB —Ferry Boat
YFD —Floating Drydock
YHB —Houseboat
YHT —Heating Scow
YM —Dredge
YPD —Floating Pile Driver
YR —Floating Workshop
YRD(H)—Drydock Workshop—Hull
YRD(M)—Drydock Workshop—Machinery
YSD —Seaplane Wreck Derrick
YSP —Salvage Pontoon

Name	Type	No.	Name	Type	No.	Name	Type	No.	Name	Type	No.
A T Middleton	APA	25	Alabama	BB	60	Almandite	PY	24	Antaeus	AS	21
Aaron Ward	DD	773	Alabaster	PYc	21	Almond	GAGL	177	Antares	AKS	3
Abbot	DD	629	Alacrity	PG	87	Alnitah	AK	127	Antelope	IX	109
Abele	YN	77	Alaska	CB	1	Aloe	YN	1	Anthedon	AS	24
Ability	PYc	28	Alatok	GYP	172	Alpine	APA	92	Anthony	DD	515
Abnaki	AT	96	Alava Bay	CVE	103	Alsea	AT	97	Anticline	YO	62
Abner Read	DD	526	Albacore	SS	218	Alshain	AKA	55	Antigua	AF	17
Absecon	AVP	23	Albatross	AM	71	Altair	AD	11	Antona	IX	133
Accelerate	ARS	30	Albemarle	AV	5	Altamaha	CVE	18	Apache	AT	67
Accentor	AMc	36	Albert W Grant	DD	649	Aludra	AK	72	Apalachee	GYT	71
Achelous	ARL	1	Albireo	AK	90	Amaranth	GAGL	201	Apogon	SS	308
Acme	AMc	61	Albuquerque	PF	7	Amarok	GYP	166	Apollo	AS	25
Acree	DE	167	Alchiba	AKA	6	Amber	PYc	6	Appalachian	AGC	1
Action	PG	86	Alcor	AR	10	Ambrose Channel	GAL	111	Aquamarine	PYc	7
Active	YT	112	Alcyone	AKA	7	America	IX	41	Aquarius	AKA	16
Active	GPC	125	Aldebaran	AF	10	Amer Legion	APA	17	Aquidneck	YFB	14
Acushnet	AT	63	Alden	DD	211	Amesbury	DE	66	Aquila	AK	47
Adamant	AMc	62	Alderamin	AK	116	Amethyst	PYc	3	Araner	IX	57
Adario	YNT	25	Alert	GPC	127	Amick	DE	168	Arapaho	AT	68
Adhara	AK	71	Alexander J Luke	DE	577	Ammen	DD	527	Arayat	IX	134
Admirable	AM	136	Alexandria	PF	18	Ammonusuk	AOG	23	Arbutus	GAGL	203
Adonis	ARL	4	Alfred Wolf	DE	544	Amsterdam	CL.	101	Archer Fish	SS	311
Adopt	AM	137	Alger	DE	101	Amycus	ARL	2	Arctic	AF	7
Adroit	AM	82	Algol	AKA	54	Anacapa	AG	49	Arcturus	AKA	1
Advance	AMc	63	Algonquin	GPG	75	Anaqua	YN	59	Ardent	AM	340
Advent	AM	83	Algorab	AKA	8	Anchor	ARS	13	Arethusa	IX	135
Aegir	AS	23	Algorma	AT	34	Ancon	AGC	4	Argo	GPC	100
Affray	AMc	112	Alhena	AKA	9	Anderson	DD	411	Argonne	AG	31
Agassiz	GPC	126	Alikula Bay	CVE	95	Andradite	PYc	11	Argus	PY	14
Agate	PYc	4	Alkaid	AK	114	Andres	DE	45	Ariadne	GPC	101
Agawam	AOG	6	Alkes	AK	110	Andrew Doria	IX	132	Arided	AK	73
Agenor	ARL	3	Allaquippa	YT	174	Andromeda	AKA	15	Ariel	AF	22
Aggressor	AMc	64	Allegheny	AT	19	Androscoggin	AOG	24	Aries	AK	51
Agile	AMc	111	Allen	DD	66	Anemone	GAGL	202	Arikara	AT	98
Ahrens	DE	575	Allen M Sumner	DD	692	Angler	SS	240	Aristaeus	ARB	1
Ailanthus	YN	57	Allentown	PF	52	Anguilla	PF	72	Arkansas	BB	33
Aivik	GYP	164	Allioth	AK	109	Annapolis	PF	15	Arluk	GYP	167
Ajax	AR	6	Alloway	YT	170	Annawan	YNT	18	Armadillo	IX	111
Aklak	GYP	168	Allthorn	YN	94	Anne Arundel	AP	76	Arneb	AKA	56
Ala	YT	139	Almaack	AKA	10	Annoy	AM	84	Aroostook	AOG	14

U. S. NAVAL VESSELS

Name	Type	No.	Name	Type	No.	Name	Type	No.	Name	Type	No.
Arrowwood	GAGL	176	Awahou	YAG	24	Barnett	APA	5	Belleville	CG	1737
Arthur L Bristol	DE	281	Aylwin	DD	355	Barney	DD	149	Belmont	CG	5004
Arundel	GYT	90	Azalea	GAGL	262	Barnstable	APA	93	Benham	DD	796
Arvek	GYP	165	Azimech	AK	124	Baron	DE	166	Bennett	DD	473
Ascension	PF	74	Azurlite	PY	22	Barracuda	SS	163	Bennington	CV	20
Ash	YN	2	Babbitt	DD	128	Barrier	AM	150	Bennion	DD	662
Asheville	PF	1	Bache	DD	470	Barry	DD	248	Benson	DD	421
Ashland	LSD	1	Badger	DD	126	Barton	DD	722	Berceau	YFB	3
Ashley	IX	83	Bagaduce	AT	21	Bashaw	SS	241	Bering Strait	AVP	34
Ashtabula	AO	51	Bagley	DD	386	Bass	SS	164	Bernadou	DD	153
Aspen	GAGL	204	Baham	AK	122	Bassett	DE	672	Beryl	PY	23
Aspro	SS	309	Bailer	YO	54	Basswood	GAGL	388	Besboro	AG	66
Asquith	YFB	42	Bailey	DD	492	Bataan	CVL	29	Besugo	SS	321
Assertive	AMc	65	Bainbridge	DD	246	Bateleur	AMc	37	Betelgeuse	AKA	11
Asterion	AK	63	Baker	DE	190	Bates	DE	68	Beverly	CG	2012
Astoria	CL	90	Balao	SS	285	Batfish	SS	310	Bibb	GPG	31
Astrolabe Bay	CVE	97	Balch	DD	363	Bath	PF	55	Biddle	DD	151
Astute	AM	148	Baldwin	DD	624	Baxter	APA	94	Big Chief	IX	101
Atak	GYP	163	Ballard	AVD	10	Baya	SS	318	Big Horn	CG	
Atalanta	GPC	102	Balm	YN	78	Bayfield	APA	33	Big Pebble	YHB	23
Atascosa	AO	66	Balsam	GAGL	62	Bayonne	PF	21	Billfish	SS	286
Atherton	DE	169	Baltimore	CA	68	Beagle	IX	112	Biloxi	CL	80
Atlanta	CL	104	Bancroft	DD	598	Beale	DD	471	Birch	CG	3011
Atlantic	GIX	271	Bang	SS	385	Bear	AG	29	Birmingham	CL	62
Atlantida	IX	108	Bangor	PF	16	Bearss	DD	654	Bisbee	PF	46
Atlas	ARL	7	Bangust	DE	739	Beatty	DD	640	Biscayne	AVP	11
Attu	CVE	102	Bannock	AT	81	Beaufort	PF	59	Bitterbush	YN	58
Atule	SS	403	Baranof	YAG	11	Beaumont	PG	60	Bittersweet	CG	1466
Aucilla	AO	56	Barataria	AVP	33	Beaver	AS	5	Bivin	DE	536
Augury	AM	149	Barb	SS	220	Bebas	DE	10	Black	DD	666
Augusta	CA	31	Barbal	SS	316	Becuna	SS	319	Black Douglas	PYc	45
Auk	AM	57	Barber	DE	161	Bedloe	GPC	128	Black Fox	YT	177
Aulick	DD	569	Barbero	SS	317	Beech	GAGL	205	Black Swan	CG	1739
Ault	DD	698	Barberry	GAGL	294	Belfast	PF	35	Blackfin	SS	322
Auriga	AK	98	Barbet	AMc	38	Belknap	AVD	8	Blackfish	SS	221
Aurora	GPC	103	Baretta	YN	60	Bell	DD	587	Blackhaw	GAGL	390
Austin	DE	15	Barker	DD	213	Bellatrix	AKA	3	Blackhawk	AD	9
Avenge	AMc	66	Barnegat	AVP	10	Belle Grove	LSD	2	Blackrock	GYP	367
Avocet	AVP	4	Barnegat	GAL	79	Belleau Wood	CVL	24	Blackthorn	GAGL	391
Awa	SS	409	Barnes	CVE	20	Bellefonte	CG	4996	Blair	DE	147

Name	Type	No.	Name	Type	No.	Name	Type	No.	Name	Type	No.
Blakeley	DD	150	Bostwick	DE	103	Broome	DD	210	Cabrilla	SS	288
Blanchard	GPYc	369	Bountiful	AH	10	Brough	DE	148	Cacapon	AO	52
Blanco	GPYc	343	Boutwell	GPC	130	Brown	DD	546	Cachalot	SS	170
Blaze	GSC	336	Bowditch	AGS	4	Brownson	DD	518	Cache	AO	67
Blenny	SS	324	Bowdoin	IX	50	Brownsville	PF	10	Cactus	GAGL	270
Blessman	DE	69	Bowers	DE	637	Brunswick	PF	68	Caddo	GYP	174
Block Island	CVE	21	Bowfin	SS	287	Brush	DD	745	Caelum	AK	106
Blower	SS	325	Bowstring	GSC	365	Bryant	DD	665	Cahaba	AO	82
Blue	DD	744	Boxwood	YN	3	Bucareli Bay	CVE	98	Cahokia	YT	135
Blue Dolphin	IX	65	Boyd	DD	544	Buchanan	DD	484	Cahoone	GPC	131
Blue Jay	AMc	23	Boyle	DD	600	Buckeye	YN	8	Caiman	SS	323
Blue Jay	YDT	6	Brackett	DE	41	Buckley	DE	51	Caladesi	YFB	39
Blue Ridge	AGC	2	Bradford	DD	545	Buckthorn	YN	9	Calamares	AF	18
Blueback	SS	326	Braine	DD	630	Bugara	SS	331	Calamus	AOG	25
Bluebird	AM	72	Bramble	GAGL	392	Bull	DE	693	Calcaterra	DE	390
Bluefish	SS	222	Brambling	AMc	39	Bullard	DD	660	Caldwell	DD	605
Bluegill	SS	242	Brant	ARS	32	Bullfinch	AM	66	Caliente	AO	53
Blunts Reef	GAL	100	Brave	IX	78	Bullhead	SS	332	California	BB	44
Boarfish	SS	327	Brazos	AO	4	Bullwheel	YO	46	Calistoga	YFB	21
Bobolink	AT	131	Bream	SS	243	Bulmer	DD	222	Callaghan	DD	792
Bodega	GYP	342	Breckenridge	DD	148	Bulwark	AMc	68	Callaway	APA	35
Boggs	DMS	3	Breeman	DE	104	Bumper	SS	333	Calumet	GYT	86
Bogue	CVE	9	Breese	DM	18	Bunch	DE	694	Calvert	APA	32
Boise	CL	47	Brennan	DE	13	Bunker Hill	CV	17	Calypso	GPC	104
Bold	AMc	67	Brenton Reef	GAL	102	Buoyant	AM	153	Camanga	AG	42
Bolivar	APA	34	Breton	CVE	23	Burden R Hastings	DE	19	Cambria	APA	36
Bomazeen	YT	238	Briareus	AR	12	Burke	DE	215	Cambridge	CA	126
Bombard	AM	151	Bridge	AF	1	Burleigh	APA	95	Camden	IX	42
Bond	AM	153	Bridgeport	PF	58	Burlington	PF	51	Camel	IX	113
Bonefish	SS	223	Brier	GAGL	299	Burns	DD	588	Camellia	GAGL	206
Bonham	GPC	129	Bright	DE	747	Burrfish	SS	312	Camp	DE	251
Bonita	SS	165	Brill	SS	330	Burrows	DE	105	Campbell	GPG	32
Bonneville	GIX	375	Briska	PG	80	Bush	DD	529	Canary	AMc	25
Boone	GSC	335	Brister	DE	327	Bushnell	AS	15	Canasatego	YNT	6
Bootes	AK	99	Broadbill	AM	58	Butler	DD	636	Canberra	CA	70
Booth	DE	170	Brock	DE	234	Butternut	YN	4	Candid	AM	154
Boreas	AF	8	Bronco	GYP	340	Buttonwood	GAGL	306	Canfield	DE	262
Borum	DE	790	Bronstein	DE	189	Cabana	DE	260	Cannon	DE	99
Boston	GAL	81	Brooklyn	CL	40	Cable	ARS	19	Canotia	YN	66
Boston	CA	69	Brooks	APD	10	Cabot	CVL	28	Canonicus	YT	187

U. S. NAVAL VESSELS

Name	Type	No.	Name	Type	No.	Name	Type	No.	Name	Type	No.
Capable	AM	155	Catbird	AM	68	Charleston	PG	51	Chiwaukum	AOG	26
Cape Esperance	CVE	88	Catclaw	YN	81	Charlotte	PF	60	Chiwawa	AO	68
Capelin	SS	289	Cates	DE	763	Charlottsville	PF	25	Choctaw	AT	70
Capella	AK	13	Catoctin	AGC	5	Charr	SS	328	Choptank	YT	36
Caperton	DD	650	Catskill	AP	106	Charrette	DD	581	Chowanoc	AT	100
Capitaine	SS	336	Caution	AM	158	Chas F Hughes	DD	428	Christiana	YAG	32
Capps	DD	550	Cavalier	APA	37	Chas Greer	DE	23	Christopher	DE	100
Capricornus	AKA	57	Cavalla	SS	244	Chase	DE	158	Chubb	SS	329
Captivate	AM	156	Cebu	ARG	6	Chatelain	DE	149	Cimarron	AO	22
Captor	PYc	40	Cecil	APA	96	Chatot	AT	167	Cinchona	YN	7
Caracara	AMc	40	Cedar	GAGL	207	Chattanooga	PF	65	Cincinnati	CL	6
Caravan	AM	157	Celeno	AK	76	Chatterer	AMc	16	Cisco	SS	290
Card	CVE	11	Celtic	IX	137	Chauncey	DD	667	Citrus	GAGL	200
Cardinal	AM	67	Centaurus	AKA	17	Chekilli	YT	175	Clamour	AM	160
Carib	AT	82	Cepheus	AKA	18	Chemung	AO	30	Clamp	ARS	33
Caribou	IX	114	Cero	SS	225	Chenango	CVE	28	Clarence K Bronson	DD	668
Carina	AK	74	Cetus	AK	77	Cheng Ho	IX	52	Clark	DD	361
Carlson	DE	9	Chachalaca	AMc	41	Chepachet	AO	78	Claxton	DD	571
Carmick	DD	493	Chaffee	DE	230	Cherokee	AT	66	Clay	APA	39
Carnelian	PY	19	Chaffinch	AM	81	Chesapeake Bay	GAL	116	Clemson	DD	186
Carolita	PYc	38	Chain	ARS	20	Chester	CA	27	Cleveland	CL	55
Carondelet	IX	136	Chalcedony	PYc	16	Chestnut	YN	6	Cliffrose	YN	61
Carrabasset	GAT	55	Challenge	YT	126	Chetco	ASR	12	Climax	AM	161
Carroll	DE	171	Chambers	DE	391	Chew	DD	106	Cloues	DE	265
Carson City	PF	50	Champion	AM	314	Chewink	ASR	3	Clover	GAGL	292
Carter Hall	LSD	3	Champlin	DD	601	Chickadee	AM	59	Clytie	AS	26
Cartigan	GPC	132	Chandeleur	AV	10	Chickasaw	AT	83	Coates	DE	685
Casablanca	CVE	55	Chandler	DMS	99	Chicopee	AO	34	Cobb	GPG	181
Cascade	AD	16	Change	AM	159	Chief	AM	315	Cobbler	SS	344
Casco	AVP	12	Chanticleer	ASR	23	Chikaskia	AO	54	Cobia	SS	245
Case	DD	370	Chaparral	GAGL	178	Childs	AVD	1	Cockatoo	AMc	8
Casinghead	YO	47	Chapin Bay	CVE	99	Chilton	APA	38	Cockenoe	YNT	15
Casper	PF	12	Chara	AKA	58	Chimango	AMc	42	Cockrill	DE	398
Cassin	DD	372	Charger	CVE	30	Chinaberry	YN	82	Cocopa	AT	101
Cassin Young	DD	793	Charles Ausburn	DD	570	Chincoteague	AVP	24	Cod	SS	224
Cassiopeia	AK	75	Charles Carroll	APA	28	Chinook	GYT	96	Cofer	DE	208
Castle Rock	AVP	35	Charles J Badger	DD	657	Chinquapin	YN	12	Coffman	DE	191
Castor	AKS	1	Charles Lawrence	DE	53	Chipola	AO	63	Coghlan	DD	606
Catalpa	YN	5	Charles R Ware	DE	547	Chippewa	AT	69	Cogswell	DD	651
Catawba	YT	32	Charles S Sperry	DD	697	Chivo	SS	341	Colahan	DD	658

Name	Type	No.	Name	Type	No.	Name	Type	No.	Name	Type	No.
Cole	DD	155	Coos Bay	AVP	25	Cree	AT	84	Dale	DD	353
Colfax	GPC	133	Copahee	CVE	12	Crescent City	APA	21	Dale W Peterson	DE	337
Colhoun	DD	801	Cor Caroli	AK	91	Crevalle	SS	291	Dallas	DD	199
Colington	YFB	43	Coral Sea	CVE	57	Croaker	SS	246	Daly	DD	519
Colleen	PYc	27	Corbesier	DE	106	Croatan	CVE	25	Damon M Cummings	DE	643
Colorado	BB	45	Corbitant	YT	354	Crocus	GAGL	210	Daniel	DE	335
Columbia	CL	56	Core	CVE	13	Cronin	DE	107	Daniel T Griffin	DE	54
Columbia River	GAL	93	Corkwood	YN	63	Crosby	APD	17	Danmark	GIX	283
Columbine	GAGL	208	Cormorant	AT	133	Cross Rip	GAL	96	Daphne	GPC	106
Comanche	GPG	76	Cornel	YN	64	Crossbill	AMc	9	Darby	DE	218
Combat	AMc	69	Cornfield Point	GAL	118	Crouter	DE	11	Daring	AM	87
Comfort	AH	6	Coronado	PF	38	Crowley	DE	303	Darter	SS	227
Compel	AM	162	Corpus Christi	PF	44	Crownblock	YO	48	Dash	AM	88
Competent	AM	316	Corregidor	CVE	58	Crusader	ARS	2	Dashiell	DD	659
Conanicut	YFB	15	Corry	DD	463	Crux	AK	115	Dauntless	PG	61
Conant	GYP	320	Corson	AVP	37	Crystal	PY	25	Dauphin	APA	97
Conasauga	AOG	15	Corvina	SS	226	Culebra Island	ARG	7	Davenport	PF	69
Concise	AM	163	Cosmos	GAGL	293	Cumberland	IX	8	David W Taylor	DD	551
Concord	CL	10	Cossatot	AO	77	Cumberland Sound	AV	17	Davis	DD	395
Condor	AMc	14	Cotinga	AMc	43	Cummings	DD	365	Davison	DD	618
Conflict	AM	85	Cotten	DD	669	Curb	ARS	21	Day	DE	225
Congaree	IX	84	Cottonwood	GAGL	209	Curlew	AM	69	Dayton	CL	105
Conifer	GAGL	301	Coucal	ASR	8	Current	ARS	22	Dearborn	PF	33
Conklin	DE	439	Counsel	AM	165	Currier	DE	700	Decatur	DD	341
Conner	DD	582	Courage	PG	70	Currituck	AV	7	Decker	DE	47
Connolly	DE	306	Courier	AMc	72	Curtiss	AV	4	Deede	DE	263
Conqueror	AMc	70	Courlan	AMc	44	Cushing	DD	797	Defense	AM	317
Conquest	AMc	71	Courser	AMc	32	Custer	APA	40	Defiance	AMc	73
Constant	AM	86	Covington	PF	56	Cuttlefish	SS	171	Degrasse	AP	164
Constellation	IX	20	Cowanesque	AO	79	Cuyahoga	GPC	157	Dehaven	DD	727
Constitution	IX	21	Cowell	DD	547	Cuyama	AO	3	Deimos	AK	78
Control	AM	164	Cowie	DD	632	Cyane	GPC	105	Dekanawida	YT	334
Converse	DD	509	Cowpens	CVL	25	Cygnus	AF	23	Dekanisora	YT	252
Conway	DD	507	Crane	DD	109	Cymophane	PYc	26	Dekaury	YT	178
Cony	DD	508	Crane Ship 1	AB	1	Cypress	GAGL	211	Delbert W Halsey	DE	310
Conyngham	DD	371	Crater	AK	70	Cyrene	AGP	13	Delegate	AM	217
Cook Inlet	AVP	36	Craven	DD	382	Cythera	PY	31	Deliver	ARS	23
Coolbaugh	DE	217	Crawford	GPC	134	Dace	SS	247	Delong	DE	684
Cooner	DE	172	Cread	DE	227	Dade	APA	99	Delphinus	AF	24
Cooper	DD	695	Creamer	DE	308	Dahlgren	DD	187	Delta	AR	9

Name	Type	No.	Name	Type	No.	Name	Type	No.	Name	Type	No.
Demand	AMc	74	Donaldson	DE	44	Eberle	DD	430	Emery	DE	28
Dempsey	DE	26	Doneff	DE	49	Ebert	DE	768	Emmons	DD	457
Denebola	AD	12	Donnell	DE	56	Ebony	YN	10	Emporia	PF	28
Dennis	DE	405	Doran	DD	634	Echo	IX	95	Enceladus	AK	80
Dent	APD	9	Dorothea L Dix	AP	67	Edenshaw	YT	459	Endicott	DD	495
Denver	CL	58	Dorsey	DMS	1	Edison	DD	439	Endurance	AMc	77
Derrick	YO	59	Dortch	DD	670	Edmonds	DE	406	Endymion	ARL	9
Despatch	IX	2	Douglas L Howard	DE	138	Edsall	DE	129	Engage	AM	93
Despite	AM	89	Dour	AM	223	Edwards	DD	619	England	DE	635
Detector	AMc	75	Dover	IX	30	Edwards	GYP	357	English	DD	696
Detroit	CL	8	Dow	GYP	353	Edward C Daly	DE	17	Engstrom	DE	50
Devastator	AM	318	Downes	DD	375	Edwin A. Howard	DE	346	Enhance	AM	228
Develin	AMc	45	Doyen	APA	1	Eel	SS	354	Enoree	AO	69
Devilfish	SS	292	Doyle	DD	494	Effective	AM	92	Enright	DE	216
Dewees	YFB	37	Draco	AK	79	Egeria	ARL	8	Ensenada	YAG	23
Dewey	DD	349	Dragonet	SS	293	Egret	AMc	24	Enterprise	CV	6
Dextrous	AM	341	Drayton	DD	366	Eichenberger	DE	202	Epanow	YT	275
Diamond Shoal	GAL	105	Driller	YO	61	Eisele	DE	34	Epping Forest	LSD	4
Dickerson	APD	21	Drum	SS	228	Eisner	DE	192	Equity	AM	229
Didrickson Bay	CVE	100	Du Page	APA	41	El Cano	IX	79	Erben	DD	631
Diligence	GPC	135	Duane	GPG	33	El Paso	PF	41	Ericsson	DD	440
Diodon	SS	349	Dubuque	PG	17	Elden	DE	264	Eridanus	AK	92
Dione	GPC	107	Duffy	DE	27	Elder	YN	15	Escalante	AO	70
Dionne	DE	261	Duluth	CL	87	Eldridge	DE	173	Escambia	AO	80
Diphda	AKA	59	Dunlap	DD	384	Electra	AKA	4	Escape	ARS	6
Direct	AM	90	Dupont	DD	152	Eliz C Stanton	AP	69	Escatawpa	AOG	27
Discoverer	ARS	3	Durant	DE	389	Elk	IX	115	Escolar	SS	294
Disdain	AM	222	Dutchess	APA	98	Elkhorn	AOG	7	Esselen	AT	147
Diver	ARS	5	Duxbury Bay	AVP	38	Ellet	DD	398	Essex	CV	9
Dix	GPC	136	Dwyn Wen	IX	58	Elliot	DMS	4	Esteem	AM	230
Dixie	AD	14	Dynamic	AM	91	Ellis	DD	154	Etamin	AK	93
Dobbin	AD	3	Dyson	DD	572	Ellyson	DD	454	Eucalyptus	YN	11
Dobler	DE	48	E A Poe	IX	103	Elm	CG	3026	Eugene	PF	40
Dogwood	GAGL	259	E G Chase	DE	16	Elmore	APA	42	Eunaw	IX	85
Dohasan	YT	335	Eager	AM	224	Elokomin	AO	55	Euphane	GYP	360
Doherty	DE	14	Earl K Olsen	DE	765	Elusive	AM	225	Euryale	AS	22
Dolomi Bay	CVE	101	Earl V Johnson	DE	702	Ely	DE	309	Evans	DD	552
Dolphin	SS	169	Earle	DD	635	Embattle	AM	226	Evansville	PF	70
Dominant	AMc	76	Eastwind	GPG	279	Embroil	AM	227	Evarts	DE	5
Donacona	YNT	7	Eaton	DD	510	Emerald	PYc	1	Evea	YT	458

Name	Type	No.	Name	Type	No.	Name	Type	No.	Name	Type	No.
Event	AM	231	Fixity	AM	235	Fremont	APA	44	Gen E T Collins	AP	147
Everett	PF	8	Flaherty	DE	135	Frost	DE	144	Gen G M Randall	AP	115
Evergreen	GAGL	295	Flame	AM	236	Frosty Bay	CVE	112	Gen G O Squire	AP	130
Eversale	DE	404	Flamingo	AMc	22	Frybarger	DE	705	Gen H B Freeman	AP	143
Ewing	GPC	137	Flasher	SS	249	Frying Pan Shoals	GAL	115	Gen H F Hodges	AP	144
Excel	AM	94	Fleming	DE	32	Fullam	DD	474	Gen H L Scott	AP	136
Execute	AM	232	Fletcher	DD	445	Fuller	APA	7	Gen H W Butner	AP	113
Exploit	AM	95	Flicker	AM	70	Fulmar	AMc	46	Gen Harry Taylor	AP	145
Extractor	ARS	15	Flier	SS	251	Fulton	AS	11	Gen J H McRae	AP	149
Extricate	ARS	16	Flint	CL	97	Fury	PG	69	Gen J R Brooke	AP	132
F Nightingale	AP	70	Florican	ASR	9	G E Badger	AVD	3	Gen John Pope	AP	110
Facility	AM	233	Flounder	SS	251	Gabilan	SS	252	Gen M B Stewart	AP	140
Fair	DE	35	Floyds Bay	AVP	40	Galatea	GPC	108	Gen M L Hersey	AP	148
Falcon	ASR	2	Flusser	DD	368	Galaxy	IX	54	Gen M M Patrick	AP	150
Falgout	DE	324	Flying Fish	SS	229	Gallant	PYc	29	Gen O H Ernst	AP	133
Fancy	AM	234	Fogg	DE	57	Gallup	PF	47	Gen R E Callen	AP	139
Fanning	DD	385	Fomalhaut	AKA	5	Gambier Bay	CVE	7	Gen R L Howze	AP	134
Fanshaw Bay	CVE	70	Foote	DD	510	Gamble	DM	15	Gen S D Sturgis	AP	137
Farenholt	DD	491	Force	AM	99	Gandy	DE	764	Gen T H Bliss	AP	131
Farquhar	DE	139	Foreman	DE	633	Gansevoort	DD	608	Gen W C Langfitt	AP	151
Farragut	DD	348	Formoe	DE	509	Gantner	DE	60	Gen W F Hase	AP	146
Faunce	GPC	138	Forrest	DD	461	Ganymede	AK	104	Gen W L Black	AP	135
Favorite	IX	45	Forster	DE	334	Gar	SS	206	Gen Will A Mann	AP	112
Fayette	APA	43	Forsyth	PF	102	Gardiners Bay	AVP	39	Gen Will Mitchell	AP	114
Fechteler	DE	157	Forsythia	GAGL	63	Garland	AM	238	Gendreau	DE	639
Feland	APA	11	Fortify	AM	237	Garnet	PYc	15	General Greene	GPC	140
Fern	GAGL	304	Forward	GIX	160	Gary	DE	326	Genesee	AOG	8
Fessenden	DE	142	Foss	DE	59	Gatling	DD	671	Gentian	GAGL	290
Fidelity	AM	96	Fowler	DE	222	Gato	SS	212	George	DE	697
Fieberling	DE	640	Fox	DD	234	Gauger	YO	55	George Clymer	APA	27
Fierce	AM	97	Frament	DE	677	Gayety	AM	239	George F Elliott	AP	105
Finback	SS	230	Francis M Robinson	DE	220	Gaymier	DE	751	George W Ingram	DE	62
Finch	DE	328	Frankford	DD	497	Gazelle	IX	116	Geronimo	YT	119
Fir	GAGL	212	Franklin	CV	13	Gear	ARS	34	Gherardi	DD	637
Fire Island	GAL	114	Franks	DD	554	Gemini	AP	75	Giansar	AK	111
Firecrest	AMc	33	Frazier	DD	607	Gemsbok	IX	117	Gillespie	DD	609
Firm	AM	98	Fred Funston	APA	89	Gen A E Anderson	AP	111	Gillette	DE	681
Fiske	DE	143	Frederick C Davis	DE	136	Gen A W Greely	AP	141	Gilligan	DE	508
Fitch	DD	462	Frederick Lee	GPC	139	Gen C G Morton	AP	138	Gillis	AVD	12
Five Fathom Bank	GAL	108	Freedom	IX	43	Gen C H Muir	AP	142	Gilmer	APD	11

U. S. NAVAL VESSELS

Name	Type	No.	Name	Type	No.	Name	Type	No.	Name	Type	No.
Gilmore	DE	18	Gresham	GPG	85	Haida	GPG	45	Haverfield	DE	393
Giraffe	IX	118	Greyhound	IX	106	Hailey	DD	556	Hawk	AM	133
Girasol	PY	27	Gridley	DD	380	Haines	DE	792	Hawkbill	SS	366
Gladiator	AM	319	Griffin	AS	13	Haiglar	YT	327	Hawthorn	GAGL	215
Gleaves	DD	423	Griswold	DE	7	Hake	SS	256	Hayter	DE	212
Glendale	PF	36	Grosbeak	AMc	19	Halawa	AOG	12	Hazard	AM	240
Glennon	DD	620	Groton	PF	29	Hale	DD	642	Hazel	YN	24
Gloria Dalton	IX	70	Grouper	SS	214	Half Moon	AVP	26	Hazelwood	DD	531
Gloucester	PF	22	Grouse	AMc	12	Halfbeak	SS	352	Healy	DD	672
Goff	DD	247	Groves	DE	543	Halfford	DD	480	Heath Hen	AMc	6
Gold Star	AG	12	Growler	SS	215	Halibut	SS	232	Hector	AR	7
Goldcrest	AM	80	Grumium	AK	112	Hall	DD	583	Heed	AM	100
Golden Gate	GYT	94	Guadalcanal	CVE	60	Halligan	DD	584	Heekon	YT	141
Goldenrod	GAGL	213	Guadalupe	AO	32	Halloran	DE	305	Heermann	DD	532
Goldfinch	AM	77	Gualala	AOG	28	Halsey Powell	DD	686	Helm	DD	388
Goldsborough	AVD	5	Guardfish	SS	217	Hambleton	DD	455	Hemlock	GAGL	217
Golet	SS	361	Guavina	SS	362	Hamilton	DMS	18	Hemminger	DE	746
Goshawk	AM	79	Gudgeon	SS	211	Hamlin	AV	15	Hen and Chickens	GAL	86
Gould I S	YFB	31	Guest	DD	472	Hammann	DE	131	Henrico	APA	45
Governor	AMc	82	Guide	AMc	83	Hammerhead	SS	364	Henry A Wiley	DD	749
Grackle	AM	73	Guinivere	IX	67	Hammondsport	AKV	2	Henry R Kenyon	DE	683
Grand Forks	PF	11	Guitarro	SS	363	Hamul	AD	20	Henry T Allen	APA	15
Grand Island	PF	14	Gulfport	PF	20	Hancock	CV	19	Herald	AM	101
Grand Rapids	PF	31	Gull	AM	74	Handkerchief	GAL	98	Herbert C Jones	DE	137
Grapple	ARS	7	Gumtree	YN	13	Hannibal	AG	1	Herbert	APD	22
Grasp	ARS	24	Gunason	DE	795	Haraden	DD	585	Hercules	AK	41
Grayback	SS	208	Gunnel	SS	253	Harder	SS	257	Hermes	GPC	109
Grayling	SS	209	Gunston Hall	LSD	5	Hardhead	SS	365	Hermitage	AP	54
Grayson	DD	435	Gurnard	SS	254	Harding	DD	625	Herndon	DD	638
Green I	YFB	32	Gustafson	DE	182	Harjurand	ARS	31	Heroic	AMc	84
Greenbrier	GAGL	214	Guyandot	AOG	16	Harold C Thomas	DE	21	Heron	AVP	2
Greene	AVD	13	Gwin	DD	772	Harmon	DE	678	Herring	SS	233
Greenlet	ASR	10	Gyatt	DE	550	Harriet Lane	GPC	141	Herzog	DE	178
Greenling	SS	213	H F Liggett	APA	14	Harris	APA	2	Heywood	APA	6
Greensboro	PF	101	H R Humphreys	GYP	325	Harrison	DD	573	Heywood L Edwards	DD	663
Greenwich Bay	AVP	41	Hackberry	YN	20	Harry E Hubbard	DD	748	Hiawatha	YT	265
Greenwood	DE	679	Hackleback	SS	295	Harry Lee	APA	10	Hibiscus	GAGL	218
Greer	DD	145	Haddo	SS	255	Hartford	IX	13	Hickory	GAGL	219
Gregory	DD	802	Haddock	SS	231	Harveson	DE	316	Hickox	DD	673
Greiner	DE	37	Haggard	DD	555	Hatfield	DD	231	Hidatsa	AT	102

Name	Type	No.	Name	Type	No.	Name	Type	No.	Name	Type	No.
Highland Light	IX	48	Howard F Clark	DE	533	Independence	CVL	22	Jaguar	IX	120
Hilarity	AM	241	Howard W Gilmore	AS	16	Indiana	BB	58	Jallao	SS	368
Hilary P Jones	DD	427	Howard	DMS	7	Indianapolis	CA	35	James E Craig	DE	201
Hilbert	DE	742	Howorth	DD	592	Indicative	AM	250	James O'Hara	APA	90
Hill	DE	141	Hubbard	DE	211	Indus	AKN	1	Jamestown	AGP	3
Hilo	AGP	2	Hudson	DD	475	Industry	AMc	86	Janssen	DE	396
Hingham	PF	30	Hudson	GYT	87	Inflict	AM	251	Jarvis	DD	799
Hissem	DE	400	Hughes	DD	410	Ingersoll	DD	652	Jason	ARH	1
Hitchiti	AT	103	Hulbert	AVD	6	Ingham	GPG	35	Jasper	PYc	13
Hiwassee	AOG	29	Hull	DD	350	Ingraham	DD	694	Jawfish	SS	356
Hobart Bay	CVE	113	Humboldt	AVP	21	Instill	AM	252	Jeffers	DD	621
Hobby	DD	610	Hummingbird	AMc	26	Intensity	PG	93	Jenkins	DD	447
Hobson	DD	464	Humphreys	APD	12	Intrepid	CV	11	Jenks	DE	665
Hodges	DE	231	Hunt	DD	674	Intrigue	AM	253	Jesse Rutherford	DE	347
Hoe	SS	258	Huron	PF	19	Invade	AM	254	Jet	PYc	20
Hoel	DD	533	Hurst	DE	250	Iolite	PYc	41	Jewel	YFB	22
Hoga	YT	146	Huse	DE	145	Iowa	BB	61	Jicarilla	AT	104
Hogan	DMS	6	Hutchins	DD	476	Ira Jeffery	DE	63	John C Butler	DE	339
Hoggatt Bay	CVE	75	Hutchinson	PF	45	Irene Forsyte	IX	93	John D Edwards	DD	216
Holder	DE	401	Hyacinth	GAGL	221	Iris	GAGL	395	John D Ford	DD	228
Holland	AS	3	Hyades	AF	28	Ironwood	GAGL	297	John D Henley	DD	553
Hollis	DE	794	Hydrographer	AGS	2	Irwin	DD	794	John Hood	DD	655
Holly	YN	14	Hyman	DD	732	Isabel	PY	10	John J Powers	DE	528
Hollyhock	GAGL	220	Hyperion	AK	107	Isherwood	DD	520	John J Van Buren	DE	753
Holton	DE	703	Ibex	IX	119	Iuka	AT	37	John M Bermingham	DE	530
Honolulu	CL	48	Ibis	AM	134	Iwana	YT	272	John M Howard	IX	75
Hope	AH	7	Icarus	GPC	110	Izard	DD	589	John Q Roberts	DE	235
Hopewell	DD	681	Icefish	SS	367	J Douglas Blackwood	DE	219	John Rodgers	DD	574
Hopi	AT	71	Idaho	BB	42	J F Bell	APA	16	Johnston	DD	557
Hopkins	DMS	13	Ideal	AMc	85	J Fred Talbott	DD	156	Jordan	DE	204
Hopocan	YNT	1	Ilex	GAGL	222	J M Howard	IX	75	Joseph E Campbell	DE	70
Hopping	DE	155	Illinois	BB	65	J R Y Blakely	DE	140	Jouett	DD	396
Hoptree	YN	83	Impeccable	AM	320	J Richard Ward	DE	243	Joyce	DE	317
Hoquiam	PF	5	Impetuous	PYc	46	J T Dickman	APA	13	Jubilant	AM	255
Hornbeam	GAGL	394	Implicit	AM	246	Jacamar	AMc	47	Junaluska	YT	176
Hornet	CV	12	Improve	AM	247	Jack	SS	259	Juneau	CL	119
Housatonic	AO	35	Impulse	PG	68	Jack Miller	DE	410	Juniata	IX	77
Houston	CL	81	Incessant	AM	248	Jack W Wilke	DE	800	Juniper	GAGL	224
Hovey	DMS	11	Inch	DE	146	Jackson	GPC	142	Jupiter	AK	43
Howard D Crow	DE	252	Incredible	AM	249	Jacob Jones	DE	130	Kadashan Bay	CVE	76

U. S. NAVAL VESSELS

Name	Type	No.	Name	Type	No.	Name	Type	No.	Name	Type	No.
Kailua	IX	71	Kildeer	AMc	21	Lamar	APA	47	Leonard Wood	APA	12
Kalamazoo	AOG	30	Killen	DD	593	Lamberton	DMS	2	Leonis	AK	128
Kalinin Bay	CVE	68	Kilty	APD	15	Lamons	DE	743	Leopard	IX	122
Kalk	DD	611	Kimball	GPC	143	Lamprey	SS	372	Leopold	DE	319
Kalmia	AT	23	Kimberly	DD	521	Lamson	DD	367	Leslie L B Knox	DE	580
Kaloli	AOG	13	King	DD	242	Lance	AM	257	Lesuth	AK	125
Kanawha	AOG	31	Kingbird	AMc	56	Lancetfish	SS	296	Leutze	DD	481
Kane	APD	18	Kingfish	SS	234	Lancewood	YN	67	Levy	DE	162
Kangaroo	IX	121	Kingfisher	AT	135	Lang	DD	399	Lewis	DE	535
Kankakee	AO	39	Kinzer	DE	232	Langley	CVL	27	Lewis Hancock	DD	675
Kansas City	CA	128	Kiowa	AT	72	Laning	DE	159	Lexington	CV	16
Kasaan Bay	CVE	69	Kirkpatrick	DE	318	Lansdale	DD	426	Leyte	ARG	8
Kaskaskia	AO	27	Kishwaukee	AOG	9	Lansdowne	DD	486	Liberator	AMc	87
Katlian	YNT	16	Kite	AM	75	Lansing	DE	388	Liberty Belle	IX	72
Kaula	AG	33	Kitkun Bay	CVE	71	Lapon	SS	260	Libra	AKA	12
Kaw	GYT	61	Kitty Hawk	AKV	1	Lapwing	AVP	1	Liddle	DE	206
Kaweah	AO	15	Klamath	GPG	66	Laramie	AO	16	Lilac	GAGL	227
Kearny	DD	432	Knapp	DD	653	Larch	YN	16	Limpkin	AMc	48
Kearsarge	CV	33	Knave	AM	256	Lardner	DD	487	Linden	GAGL	228
Keith	DE	241	Knight	DD	633	Lark	AM	21	Lindenwald	LSD	6
Kendrick	DD	611	Knox	APA	46	Larkspur	GAGL	226	Lindsey	DD	771
Kenmore	AP	162	Knoxville	PF	64	LaSalle	AP	102	Ling	SS	297
Kennebago	AO	81	Kochab	AKS	6	Lash	PYc	31	Linnet	AM	76
Kennebec	AO	36	Kodiak	GYP	173	Lassen	AE	3	Lionfish	SS	298
Kenneth Whiting	AV	14	Kohi	YAG	27	Laub	DD	613	Lipan	AT	85
Kennison	DD	138	Koiner	DE	331	Laurel	GAGL	291	Liston	IX	92
Kentucky	BB	66	Konoka	YT	151	Lavallette	DD	448	Litchfield	DD	336
Keokuk	AKN	4	Kopara	AG	50	Lawrence	DD	250	Little	DD	803
Keosanqua	AT	38	Kraken	SS	370	Laws	DD	558	Little Joe	GYP	356
Kephart	DE	207	Kretchmer	DE	329	Lea	DD	118	Little Rock	CL	92
Keppler	DE	311	Kukui	GAGL	225	Leader	PYc	42	Livermore	DD	429
Kern	AOG	2	Kula Gulf	CVE	108	League 18	YFB	20	Livingston	AP	163
Keshena	YNT	5	Kyne	DE	744	Leary	DD	158	Lizardfish	SS	373
Kestrel	AMc	5	La Prade	DE	409	Lee Fox	DE	65	Lloyd	DE	209
Kete	SS	369	Lackawanna	AO	40	Leedstown	APA	56	Lloyd Thomas	DE	312
Kewaydin	AT	24	Lafayette	APV	4	Legare	GPC	144	Locust	YN	17
Key West	PF	17	Laffey	DD	724	Lehardy	DE	20	Loeser	DE	680
Kiasutha	YT	463	Lagarto	SS	371	Lejeune	AP	74	Logger Head	SS	374
Kickapoo	GAGL	56	Lake	DE	301	Leo	AKA	60	Logic	AM	258
Kidd	DD	661	Lake Champlain	CV	39	Leon	APA	48	Lone Wolf	YT	179

Name	Type	No.
Long Beach	PF	34
Long Island	CVE	1
Long	DMS	12
Longshaw	DD	559
Longspur	AMc	10
Lorain	PF	97
Lorikeet	AMc	49
Los Angeles	CA	135
Lotus	GAGL	229
Louisville	CA	28
Lovelace	DE	198
Lovering	DE	39
Lowe	DE	325
Lowry	DD	770
Loy	DE	160
Loyalty	AMc	88
Luce	DD	522
Lucid	AM	259
Ludlow	DD	438
Luna	AKS	7
Lunga Point	CVE	94
Lupine	GAGL	230
Luster	IX	82
Luzon	ARG	2
Lyman	DE	302
Lyman K Swenson	DD	729
Lynx	AK	100
Lyon	AP	71
Lyra	AK	101
Macabi	SS	375
Macaw	ASR	11
MacDonough	DD	351
Machias	PF	53
Mackenzie	DD	614
Mackerel	SS	204
Mackinac	AVP	13
Mackinaw	CG	1716
MacLeish	DD	220
Macomb	DD	458
Macon	PF	96
Madalan	GPYc	345
Maddox	DD	731
Madison	DD	425
Madokawando	YT	180
Madrona	GAGL	302
Magnet	AM	260
Magnolia	GAGL	231
Magpie	AMc	2
Mahan	DD	364
Mahaska	YNT	4
Mahogany	YN	18
Mahoning	GYT	91
Mahopac	AT	29
Mainstay	AM	261
Majaba	IX	102
Major	DE	796
Makassar Strait	CVE	91
Malanao	AG	44
Mallard	ASR	4
Mallow	GAGL	396
Maloy	DE	791
Malvern	IX	138
Mamo	YT	325
Manasquan	GPG	273
Manatee	AO	58
Manchester	CL	83
Manchineel	YN	73
Mango	YN	19
Mangrove	GAGL	232
Manhasset	GPG	276
Manhattan	GYT	95
Manila Bay	CVE	61
Manileno	IX	141
Manistee	YT	173
Manitou	GY2	60
Manitowoc	PF	61
Mankato	YNT	8
Manley	APD	1
Manlove	DE	36
Manning	DE	199
Mansfield	DD	728
Manta	SS	299
Manuwai	YFB	16
Manzanita	GAGL	233
Mapiro	SS	376
Maple	GAGL	234
Marabout	AMc	50
Marblehead	CL	12
Marcasite	PY	28
Marchand	DE	249
Marcus Island	CVE	77
Margaret	CG	1773
Marias	AO	57
Marigold	GAGL	235
Marin	YNT	21
Marine Angel	SMT	15
Marine Beaver	SMT	13
Marine Devil	SMT	5
Marine Dolphin	SMT	11
Marine Dragon	SMT	7
Marine Eagle	SMT	1
Marine Fox	SMT	8
Marine Hawk	SMT	9
Marine Lion	SMT	10
Marine Owl	SMT	14
Marine Panther	SMT	6
Marine Raven	SMT	2
Marine Robin	SMT	3
Marine Walrus	SMT	12
Marine Wolf	SMT	4
Marion	GPC	145
Mariposa	GAGL	397
Marita	GPY	175
Markab	AD	21
Marlin	SS	205
Martin H Ray	DE	338
Marnell	PYc	39
Marsh	DE	699
Marshall	DD	676
Marthas Vinyard	IX	97
Martin	DE	30
Marts	DE	174
Marvel	AM	262
Maryland	BB	46
Mascoma	AO	83
Mason	DE	529
Massachusetts	BB	59
Massasoit	YT	131
Mastic	YN	65
Mataco	AT	86
Matagorda	AVP	22
Mattaponi	AO	41
Mattole	AO	17
Maumee	AO	2
Mauna Loa	AE	8
Maury	DD	401
Mauvila	YT	328
Mawkaw	YT	182
Mayflower	GPG	183
Mayo	DD	422
Mayrant	DD	402
Mazama	AE	9
Mazapeta	YT	181
McAnn	DE	179
McCall	DD	400
McCalla	DD	488
McClelland	DE	750
McConnell	DE	163
McCook	DD	496
McCord	DD	534
McCormick	DD	223
McCoy Reynolds	DE	440
McDermut	DD	677
McDougal	DD	358
McFarland	DD	237
McGowan	DD	678
McKee	DD	575
McLanahan	DD	615
McLane	GPC	146
McNair	DD	679

U. S. NAVAL VESSELS

Name	Type	No.	Name	Type	No.	Name	Type	No.	Name	Type	No.
McNulty	DE	581	Micka	DE	176	Mojave	GPG	47	Murzim	AK	95
Meade	DD	602	Midas	ARB	5	Molala	AT	106	Muskallunge	SS	262
Measure	AM	263	Midway	CVE	63	Mona Island	ARG	9	Muskegon	PF	24
Medusa	AR	1	Might	PG	94	Monadnock	CM	9	Muskogee	PF	49
Megrez	AK	126	Migrant	IX	66	Monaghan	DD	354	Mustin	DD	413
Melville	AD	2	Mikanopy	YT	329	Monhegan	YFB	18	Myles C Fox	DE	546
Melvin	DD	680	Milan	YP	6	Monitor	AP	160	Namequa	YT	331
Memorable	AMc	89	Miles	DE	183	Monomoy	AG	40	Namontack	YNT	14
Memphis	CL	13	Milledgeville	PF	98	Monongahela	AO	42	Nanok	GYP	169
Mendocino	APA	100	Miller	DD	535	Monrovia	APA	31	Nantahala	AO	60
Mendota	GPG	69	Millicoma	AO	73	Monssen	DD	798	Nantucket Shoals	GAL	112
Menemsha	AG	39	Mills	DE	383	Montajk	AP	161	Naos	AK	105
Menewa	YNT	2	Milwaukee	CL	5	Montcalm	AT	39	Narcissus	GAGL	238
Menges	DE	320	Mimosa	YN	21	Monterey	CVL	26	Narkeeta	YT	133
Menhaden	SS	377	Mindanao	ARG	3	Montezuma	YT	145	Narragansett	AT	88
Menkar	AK	123	Mindoro	YAG	15	Montgomery	DM	17	Narraguagas	AOG	32
Menominee	AT	73	Mingo	SS	261	Monticello	AP	61	Narwhal	SS	167
Mentor	PYc	37	Mink	IX	123	Montour	APA	101	Nashira	AK	85
Merak	AF	21	Minneapolis	CA	36	Montpelier	CL	57	Nashville	CL	43
Mercury	AK	42	Minnehaha	YT	271	Moore	DE	240	Nassau	CVE	16
Mercy	AH	8	Minnetonka	GPG	67	Moose	IX	124	Natoma Bay	CVE	62
Meredith	DD	726	Mintaka	AK	94	Moosehead	IX	98	Naugatuck	GYT	92
Merganser	AM	135	Mirth	AM	265	Moray	SS	300	Nauset	AT	29
Merit	AMc	90	Mission Bay	CVE	59	Moreno	AT	87	Nautilus	SS	168
Mero	SS	378	Mississinewa	AO	59	Morris	GPC	147	Navesink	GYT	88
Merrill	DE	392	Mississippi	BB	41	Morris	DD	417	Navigator	YT	39
Merrimack	AO	37	Missouri	BB	63	Morrison	DD	560	Nawat	YMT	23
Mertz	DD	691	Mistletoe	GAGL	237	Mosley	DE	321	Neches	AO	47
Mervine	DD	489	Mitchell	DE	43	Motive	AM	102	Needlefish	SS	379
Mesquite	GAGL	305	Mizar	AF	12	Mt Baker	AE	4	Negwagon	YT	188
Messick	GYP	358	Mizpah	PY	29	Mount Hood	AE	11	Nehenta Bay	CVE	74
Metacom	YNT	19	Moale	DD	693	Mt Vernon	AP	22	Nellwood	GPYc	337
Metcalfe	DD	595	Mobile	CL	63	Mugford	DD	389	Nelson	DD	623
Metea	YNT	9	Mobjack	AGP	7	Mulberry	YN	22	Nemaha	GPC	148
Metha Nelson	IX	74	Mocking Bird	AMc	28	Muliphen	AKA	61	Nemasket	AOG	10
Method	AM	264	Moctobi	AT	105	Mullany	DD	528	Nemesis	GPC	111
Mettawee	AOG	17	Modoc	GPG	46	Munda	CVE	104	Neomonni	YT	349
Miami	CL	89	Moffett	DD	362	Munsee	AT	107	Neosho	AO	48
Miantonomah	CM	10	Mohawk	GPG	78	Murphy	DD	603	Nepanet	YT	189
Micawber	GPG	67	Mohican	GYT	73	Murray	DD	576	Nereus	AS	17

Name	Type	No.	Name	Type	No.	Name	Type	No	Name	Type	No.
Nerka	SS	380	North Carolina	BB	55	Ojibwa	GYT	97	Osmond Ingram	DD	255
Neshanic	AO	71	North Star	GPG	59	Okeechobee	GPG	—	Osmus	DE	701
Nestor	ARB	6	North Wind	CG65	3	Okisko	YNT	10	Osprey	AM	56
Nesutan	YT	338	Northhampton	CA	125	Oklahoma	BB	37	Ossipee	GPR	50
Neswage	YNT	17	Northland	GPG	49	Oklahoma City	CL	91	Osterhaus	DE	164
Neuendorf	DE	200	Northumberland	GYP	361	Oklawaha	AO	84	Ostrich	AMc	51
Neunzer	DE	150	Northwind	GPG	278	Olivin	PYc	22	Oswald	DE	767
Nevada	BB	36	Norton Sound	AV	11	Olympia	IX	40	Oswald A Powers	DE	542
Neville	APA	9	Notable	AM	267	Omaha	CL	4	O'Toole	DE	527
New Bedford	GAL	106	Nourmahal	PG	72	Ommaney Bay	CVE	79	Otter	DE	210
New Bedford	PF	71	Nucleus	AM	268	O'Neill	DE	188	Otterstetter	DE	244
New Haven	CL	109	Nuthatch	AM	60	Oneka	YNT	3	Otus	AS	20
New Jersey	BB	62	Nutmeg	YN	28	Ono	SS	357	Overfalls	GAL	101
New Mexico	BB	40	O 2	SS	63	Onondaga	GPG	79	Overton	APD	23
New Orleans	CA	32	O 3	SS	64	Onslow	AVP	48	Owasco	GPG	39
New York	BB	34	O 4	SS	65	Ontario	AT	13	Owen	DD	536
Newark	CL	108	O 6	SS	67	Ontonagon	AOG	36	Owl	AT	137
Newcomb	DD	586	O 7	SS	68	Onyx	PYc	5	Oyster Bay	AGP	6
Newell	DE	322	O 8	SS	69	Opal	PYc	8	Ozark	AP	107
Newman	DE	205	O 10	SS	71	Opponent	AM	269	P H Burnett	IX	104
Newport	PF	27	Oahu	ARG	5	Oracle	AM	103	Paddle	SS	263
Newton	IX	33	Oak	GAGL	239	Orange	PF	43	Paducah	PG	18
Niblack	DD	424	Oak Hill	LSD	7	Oratamin	YT	347	Pakana	AT	108
Nicholas	DD	449	Oakland	CL	95	Orca	AVP	49	Palisade	AM	270
Nicholson	DD	442	O'Bannon	DD	450	Orchid	GAGL	240	Palm	YN	23
Nields	DD	616	Oberon	AKA	14	Ordronaux	DD	617	Palmer	DMS	5
Nightingale	AMc	149	Oberrender	DE	344	Oregon City	CA	122	Palo Blanco	YN	85
Nihoa	YFB	17	O'Brien	DD	725	O'Reilly	DE	330	Palomas	IX	91
Nike	GPC	112	Observer	AMc	91	Orestes	AGP	10	Paloverde	YN	86
Nimble	AM	266	Oceanographer	AGS	3	Oriole	AT	136	Pamanset	AO	85
Niobrara	AO	72	Oceanus	ARB	2	Orion	AS	18	Pamlico	GPR	57
Nitro	AE	2	Ocelot	IX	110	Oriskany	CV	34	Pampanito	SS	383
Noa	APD	24	Ochlockonee	AOG	33	Orizaba	AP	24	Panay	AG	41
Nogak	GYP	171	Oconee	AOG	34	Orlando	PF	99	Panda	IX	125
Noka	YNT	22	Octans	AF	26	Ormsby	APA	49	Pandora	GPC	113
Nokomis	YT	142	Octorara	IX	139	Orono	YT	190	Panther	IX	105
Norfolk	CL	118	O'Flaherty	DE	340	Ortolan	ASR	5	Papaw	GAGL	308
Norma	AK	26	Ogden	PF	39	Osage	AP	108	Papaya	YN	68
Norman Scott	DD	690	Ogeechee	AOG	35	Osamekin	YT	191	Paragon	PYc	36
North	YFB	46	Oglala	ARG	1	Osceola	YT	129	Paramount	AMc	92

U. S. NAVAL VESSELS

Name	Type	No.
Parche	SS	384
Pargo	SS	264
Parker	DD	604
Parks	DE	165
Parrakeet	AMc	34
Parrott	DD	218
Partridge	AT	138
Pasadena	CL	65
Pasco	PF	6
Pasquotank	AOG	18
Pastores	AF	16
Patapsco	AOG	1
Pathfinder	AGS	1
Patoka	AO	9
Patriot	PYc	47
Patterson	DD	392
Patuxent	AO	44
Paul G Baker	DE	642
Paul Hamilton	DD	590
Paul Jones	DD	230
Pavlic	DE	669
Pawnee	AT	74
Pawtucket	YT	359
Pecos	AO	65
Peerless	AMc	93
Pegasus	AK	48
Pelias	AS	14
Pelican	AVP	6
Penetrate	AM	271
Pennewill	DE	175
Pennsylvania	BB	38
Penobscot	YT	42
Pensacola	CA	24
Peoria	PF	67
Pepperwood	YN	31
Pequot	GARC	58
Perch	SS	313
Percival	PDD	452
Peridot	PYc	18
Peril	AM	272
Perkins	DD	377
Permit	SS	178
Perry	DMS	17
Perseus	GPC	114
Perseverance	PYc	44
Persistent	PYc	48
Pert	PG	95
Pessacus	YT	192
Peterson	DE	152
Peto	SS	265
Petrof Bay	CVE	80
Pettit	DE	253
Phantom	AM	273
Phaon	ARB	3
Pheasant	AM	61
Phelps	DD	360
Phenakite	PYc	25
Philadelphia	CL	41
Philip	DD	498
Phlox	GAGL	161
Phobos	AK	129
Phoebe	AMc	57
Phoenix	CL	46
Picking	DD	685
Pictor	AF	27
Picuda	SS	382
Piedmont	AD	17
Pierce	APA	50
Pike	SS	173
Pilgrim 2	YFB	30
Pillsbury	DE	133
Pilot	AM	104
Pilotfish	SS	386
Pine	GAGL	162
Pine Island	AV	12
Pinkney	APH	2
Pinnacle	AM	274
Pinola	AT	33
Pinon	YN	87
Pintado	SS	387
Pintail	AMc	17
Pinto	AT	90
Pioneer	AM	105
Pipefish	SS	388
Pipit	AMc	1
Piranha	SS	389
Pirate	AM	275
Pitcairn	PF	85
Pittsburgh	CA	72
Pivot	AM	276
Plaice	SS	390
Planetree	GAGL	307
Platte	AO	24
Pledge	AM	277
Pleiades	AK	46
Plover	AMc	3
Pluck	AMc	94
Plunger	SS	179
Plunkett	DD	431
Pocahontas	YT	266
Pocatello	PF	9
Pochantas	GYP	362
Pocomoke	AV	9
Pocotaligo	IX	86
Pogatacut	YT	267
Pogy	SS	266
Pokagon	YT	274
Polaris	AF	11
Pollack	SS	180
Pollock Rip	GAL	110
Pollux	AKS	4
Pomfret	SS	391
Pompano	SS	181
Pompon	SS	267
Ponchatoula	AOG	38
Ponganset	AO	86
Pontiac	AF	20
Poole	DE	151
Pope	DE	134
Poplar	GAGL	241
Porcupine	IX	126
Porpoise	SS	172
Port Whangarei	YAG	85
Portage Bay	CVE	115
Portent	AM	106
Porter	DD	800
Porterfield	DD	682
Portland	CA	33
Portland	GAL	90
Portsmouth	CL	102
Portunus	AGP	4
Positive	AMc	95
Potawatomi	AT	109
Potomac	AG	25
Poughkeepsie	PF	26
Power	AMc	96
Powhatan	YT	128
Prairie	AD	15
Prairie State	IX	15
Preble	DM	20
Pres Adams	APA	19
Pres Hayes	APA	20
Pres Jackson	APA	18
Preserver	ARS	8
President Monroe	AP	104
President Polk	AP	103
Prestige	AMc	97
Preston	DD	795
Prevail	AM	107
Price	DE	332
Pride	DE	323
Prime	AM	279
Prince Georges	AP	165
Prince William	CVE	31
Princeton	CVL	23
Pringle	DD	477
Pritchett	DD	561
Procyon	AKA	2
Progress	AMc	98
Project	AM	278

Name	Type	No.	Name	Type	No.	Name	Type	No.	Name	Type	No.
Prometheus	AR	3	Raby	DE	698	Reform	AM	286	Richard W Suesens	DE	342
Protector	ARS	14	Raccoon	IX	127	Refresh	AM	287	Richey	DE	385
Proteus	AS	19	Racer	IX	100	Refuge	AH	11	Richmond	CL	9
Providence	CL	82	Radford	DD	446	Register	DE	308	Ricketts	DE	254
Prowess	AM	280	Radiant	AMc	99	Regulus	AK	14	Riddle	DE	185
Prudent	PG	96	Rail	AT	139	Rehoboth	AVP	50	Rigel	AR	11
Pruitt	DM	22	Rainier	AE	5	Reid	DD	369	Riley	DE	579
Pueblo	PF	13	Raleigh	CL	7	Reign	AM	288	Rinehart	DE	196
Puffer	SS	268	Rall	DE	304	Reina Mercedes	IX	25	Ringgold	DD	500
Puffin	AMc	29	Ralph Talbot	DD	390	Reindeer	YT	115	Rio Grande	AOG	3
Puget Sound	AV	13	Ramapo	AO	12	Reliable	AMc	100	Risk	AM	291
Pulaski	GPC	149	Rambler	GAGL	298	Reliance	GPC	150	Rival	AM	292
Pumper	YO	56	Ramona	IX	76	Relief	AH	1	Rixey	APH	3
Puritan	IX	69	Rampart	AM	282	Remey	DD	688	Rizzi	DE	537
Pursuit	AM	108	Ramsay	DM	16	Rendova	CVE	114	Roadrunner	AMc	35
Putnam	DD	757	Ramsden	DE	382	Reno	CL	96	Roamer	AF	19
Pyro	AE	1	Randolph	CV	15	Renshaw	DD	499	Roanoke	PF	93
Pyrope	PYc	17	Ranger	CV	4	Report	AM	289	Robalo	SS	273
Quapaw	AT	110	Ransom	AM	283	Reprisal	CV	35	Robert Brazier	DE	345
Quastinet	AOG	39	Rapidan	AO	18	Reproof	AM	290	Robert E Peary	DE	132
Queenfish	SS	393	Raritan	GYT	93	Republic	AP	33	Robert I Paine	DE	578
Quest	AM	281	Rasher	SS	269	Requisite	AM	109	Roberts	DE	749
Quick	DD	490	Rathburne	DD	113	Rescuer	ARS	18	Robin	AT	140
Quincy	CA	71	Raton	SS	270	Restless	PG	66	Robinson	DD	562
Quiros	IX	140	Raven	AM	55	Restorer	ARS	17	Rochambeau	AP	63
R 1	SS	78	Ray	SS	271	Retort	PYc	49	Rochester	CA	124
R 2	SS	79	Ray K Edwards	DE	237	Reuben James	DE	153	Rock	SS	274
R 4	SS	81	Raymond	DE	341	Revenge	AM	110	Rockaway	AVP	29
R 5	SS	82	Razorback	SS	394	Reybold	DE	167	Rocke	DE	197
R 6	SS	83	Reading	PF	66	Reynolds	DE	42	Rocket	AMc	101
R 7	SS	84	Ready	PG	67	Rhea	AMc	58	Rockford	PF	48
R 9	SS	86	Rebel	AM	284	Rhind	DD	404	Rocky Mount	AGC	3
R 10	SS	87	Recruit	AM	285	Rhodes	DE	384	Rodman	DD	456
R 11	SS	88	Red Cloud	YT	268	Rhododendron	GAGL	267	Roe	DD	418
R 13	SS	90	Redbud	GAGL	398	Rhodolite	PYc	19	Roller	AMc	52
R 14	SS	91	Redfin	SS	272	Rich	DE	695	Romain	IX	89
R 15	SS	92	Redfish	SS	395	Richard M Rowell	DE	403	Roncador	SS	301
R 16	SS	93	Redwood	YN	25	Richard P Leary	DD	664	Ronquil	SS	396
R 18	SS	95	Reedbird	AMc	30	Richard Peck	IX	96	Rooks	DD	804
R 20	SS	97	Reeves	DE	156	Richard S Bull	DE	402	Roper	APD	20

U. S. NAVAL VESSELS

Name	Type	No.	Name	Type	No.	Name	Type	No.	Name	Type	No.
Rose	GAGL	242	S 42	SS	153	San Carlos	AVP	51	Saugus	AP	109
Rosewood	YN	26	S 43	SS	154	San Diego	CL	53	Sauk	GYT	99
Ross	DD	563	S 44	SS	155	San Francisco	CA	38	Saunter	AM	295
Rotanin	AK	108	S 45	SS	156	San Francisco	GAGL	83	Saury	SS	189
Rotary	YO	148	S 46	SS	157	San Jacinto	CVL	30	Sausalito	PF	4
Roustabout	YO	53	S 47	SS	158	San Juan	CL	54	Savage	DE	386
Rowe	DD	564	S 48	SS	159	San Leandro	YFB	34	Savannah	CL	42
Roy O Hale	DE	336	Sabalo	SS	302	San Pablo	AVP	30	Savannah	GAL	94
Royal	AMc	102	Sabine	AO	25	San Pedro	PF	37	Savo Island	CVE	78
Royal Palm	YN	69	Sable	IX	81	Sand Lance	SS	381	Sawfish	SS	276
Ruby	PY	21	Sablefish	SS	303	Sandalwood	YN	27	Scabbardfish	SS	397
Rudderow	DE	224	Sacagawea	YT	326	Sanderling	AMc	11	Scamp	SS	277
Rudyerd Bay	CVE	81	Sacandaga	AOG	40	Sanders	DE	40	Schenck	DD	159
Ruff	AMc	59	Sacramento	PG	19	Sandpiper	AVP	9	Schley	APD	14
Runels	DE	793	Safeguard	ARS	25	Sands	APD	13	Schmitt	DE	676
Rush	GPC	151	Sagacity	AM	293	Sandusky	PF	54	Schroeder	DD	501
Russell	DD	414	Sagamore	AT	20	Sandy Bay	CVE	118	Schuylkill	AO	76
S 11	SS	116	Sage	AM	111	Sangamon	CVE	26	Sciota	AT	30
S 12	SS	117	Sagebrush	GAGL	399	Sangay	AE	10	Scorpion	SS	278
S 13	SS	118	Saginaw Bay	CVE	82	Sanibel	YFB	23	Scotland	GAL	87
S 14	SS	119	Sagita	AK	87	Santa Fe	CL	60	Scott	DE	214
S 15	SS	120	Sailfish	SS	192	Santa Rosa	YFB	33	Scout	AM	296
S 16	SS	121	Sakarissa	YT	269	Santee	CVE	29	Scranton	PF	63
S 17	SS	122	Sakatonchee	AOG	19	Sapelo	AO	11	Scrimmage	AM	297
S 18	SS	123	Salamaua	CVE	96	Sapphire	PYc	2	Scroggins	DE	799
S 20	SS	125	Salamonie	AO	26	Saranac	AO	74	Scuffle	AM	298
S 23	SS	128	Salem	CM	11	Saratoga	CV	3	Sculpin	SS	191
S 27	SS	132	Salinas	AO	19	Sardonyx	PYc	12	Sculptor	AK	103
S 28	SS	133	Salmon	SS	182	Sargent Bay	CVE	83	Sea Cat	SS	399
S 30	SS	135	Salt Lake City	CA	25	Sargo	SS	188	Sea Cloud	IX	99
S 31	SS	136	Saluda	IX	87	Sarsi	AT	111	Sea Devil	SS	400
S 32	SS	137	Salute	AM	294	Sassacus	YT	193	Sea Dog	SS	401
S 33	SS	138	Salvia	GAGL	400	Sassafras	GAGL	401	Sea Fox	SS	402
S 34	SS	139	Samaritan	AH	10	Satana	YT	270	Sea Lion	SS	315
S 35	SS	140	Sampan	YP	103	Satinleaf	YN	62	Sea Owl	SS	405
S 37	SS	142	Sampson	DD	394	Satterlee	DD	626	Sea Poacher	SS	406
S 38	SS	143	Samuel Chase	APA	26	Saturn	AK	49	Sea Robin	SS	407
S 39	SS	144	Samuel N Moore	DD	747	Saucy	PG	65	Sea Scout	PYc	43
S 40	SS	145	San Alberto Bay	CVE	116	Saufley	DD	465	Seabird	CG	1778
S 41	SS	146	San Bernadino	PG	59	Saugatuck	AO	75	Seabrook	YFB	38

Name	Type	No.	Name	Type	No.	Name	Type	No.	Name	Type	No.
Seadragon	SS	194	Shaula	AK	118	Skimmer	AMc	53	Sperry	AS	12
Seagull	AT	141	Shaw	DD	375	Skipjack	SS	184	Spica	AK	16
Seahorse	SS	304	Shawnee	GAT	54	Skipper	AMc	104	Spicewood	YN	72
Seal	SS	183	Sheboygan	PF	57	Skirmish	AM	303	Spikefish	SS	404
Searaven	SS	196	Sheehan	DE	541	Skurry	AM	304	Spindrift	IX	49
Seattle	IX	39	Sheepscott	AOG	24	Skylark	AM	63	Spokane	CL	120
Seaward	IX	60	Sheldrake	AM	62	Slater	DE	766	Spot	SS	413
Seawolf	SS	197	Sheliak	AKA	62	Sloat	DE	245	Springer	SS	414
Sebec	AO	87	Shelikof	AVP	52	Smalley	DD	565	Springfield	CL	66
Security	AMc	103	Shellbark	YN	91	Smartt	DE	257	Sproston	DD	577
Sederstrom	DE	31	Shelter	AM	301	Smith	DD	378	Spruce	GAGL	246
Sedge	GAGL	402	Shelton	DE	407	Snapper	SS	181	Spry	PG	64
Seekonk	AOG	20	Sheridan	APA	51	Snatch	ARS	27	Squanto	YT	194
Seer	AM	112	Shields	DD	596	Snohomish	GYT	98	St Andrews Bay	CVE	107
Segundo	SS	398	Shikellamy	AOG	47	Snook	SS	279	St Augustine	PG	54
Seid	DE	256	Shipley Bay	CVE	85	Snowball	YN	71	St George	AV	16
Seize	ARS	26	Shreveport	PF	23	Snowden	DE	246	St Joseph Bay	CVE	105
Selfridge	DD	357	Shrub	GAGL	244	Snyder	DE	745	St Johns River	GAL	84
Sellstrom	DE	255	Shubrick	DD	639	Solace	AH	5	St Helena	PF	86
Semmes	AG	24	Sicard	DM	21	Solar	DE	221	St Louis	CL	49
Seneca	AT	91	Sierra	AD	18	Solomons	CVE	67	St Mary	IX	144
Sennet	SS	408	Signal	IX	142	Somers	DD	381	St Paul	CA	73
Sentry	AM	299	Signet	AM	302	Sonoma	AT	12	Stack	DD	406
Sepulga	AO	20	Sigourney	DD	643	Sorrel	GAGL	296	Stadtfeld	DE	29
Sequatchie	AOG	21	Sigsbee	DD	502	South Dakota	BB	57	Staff	AM	114
Sequin	YFB	35	Silenus	AGP	11	Southard	DMS	10	Stafford	DE	411
Sequoia	GAGL	243	Silver Cloud	IX	143	Southern Seas	PY	32	Stag	IX	128
Sequoia	AG	23	Silverbell	YN	70	Southwind	GPG	280	Stagbush	YN	93
Serene	AM	300	Silverleaf	YN	92	Spadefish	SS	411	Stallion	YT	120
Serpens	AK	97	Silversides	SS	236	Spangenberg	DE	223	Stalwart	AMc	105
Serrano	AT	112	Silverstein	DE	534	Spangler	DE	696	Stamford	PF	75
Seven Seas	IX	68	Simpson	DD	221	Spar	GAGL	403	Stanly	DD	478
Severn	AO	61	Sims	DE	154	Spear	AM	322	Stansbury	DMS	8
Shabonee	YT	465	Sioux	AT	75	Spearfish	SS	190	Stanton	DE	247
Shackle	ARS	9	Siren	PY	13	Spectacle	AM	305	Starling	AM	64
Shad	SS	235	Sirius	AK	15	Spector	AM	306	Staten	YFB	36
Shamrock Bay	CVE	84	Sitka	PF	94	Speed	AM	116	Staunch	AM	307
Shangri La	CV	38	Sitkoh Bay	CVE	86	Speedwell	GAGL	245	Steady	AM	118
Shark	SS	314	Skate	SS	305	Spence	DD	512	Steamer Bay	CVE	87
Shasta	AE	6	Skenandoa	YT	336	Spencer	GPG	36	Steele	DE	8

U. S. NAVAL VESSELS

Name	Type	No.	Name	Type	No.	Name	Type	No.	Name	Type	No.
Steelhead	SS	280	Sunnadin	AT	28	Taluga	AO	62	Terror	CM	5
Stembel	DD	644	Sunset	CVE	106	Tamaha	YNT	12	Terry	DD	513
Stephanotis	YP	4	Superior	AM	311	Tamaque	YNT	20	Tesota	YN	95
Stephen McKeever	GYP	363	Surprise	PG	63	Tamarack	GAGL	248	Tetonkaha	AOG	41
Stephen Potter	DD	538	Susan B Anthony	AP	72	Tamaroa	YT	136	Texas	BB	35
Sterett	DD	407	Susquehanna	AOG	5	Tambor	SS	198	Thalassa	GPYc	348
Sterlet	SS	392	Sustain	AM	119	Tampa	GPG	48	Thatcher	DD	514
Stern	DE	187	Sutton	DE	286	Taney	GPG	37	The Sullivans	DD	537
Sterope	AK	96	Suwannee	CVE	27	Tang	SS	306	Thetis	GPC	115
Stevens	DD	479	Swallow	AM	65	Tangier	AV	8	Thetis Bay	CVE	90
Stevenson	DD	645	Swan	AVP	7	Tapacola	AMc	54	Thomas	DE	102
Stewart	DE	238	Swanson	DD	443	Taposa	YFB	1163	Thomas Stone	APA	29
Stickleback	SS	415	Swasey	DE	248	Tappahannock	AO	43	Thomason	DE	203
Stingray	SS	186	Swatane	YT	344	Tarazed	AF	13	Thompson	DD	627
Stockdale	DE	399	Sway	AM	120	Tarbell	DD	142	Thorn	DD	647
Stockham	DD	683	Swearer	DE	186	Tarpon	SS	175	Thornback	SS	418
Stockton	DD	646	Sweetbrier	GAGL	405	Tatnuck	AT	27	Thornton	AVD	11
Stoddard	DD	566	Sweetgum	GAGL	309	Tatoosh	YAG	1	Thos Jefferson	APA	30
Stone Horse Shoal	GAL	53	Swenning	DE	394	Tattnall	APD	19	Threadfin	SS	410
Storis	GPC	38	Swerve	AM	121	Tatum	DE	789	Threat	AM	124
Strategy	AM	308	Swift	AM	122	Taupata	YAG	26	Thresher	SS	200
Stratford	AP	41	Swiftsure Bank	GAL	113	Taurus	AF	25	Thrush	AVP	3
Straub	DE	181	Swivel	ARS	36	Taussig	DD	746	Thuban	AKA	19
Straus	DE	408	Swordfish	SS	193	Tautog	SS	199	Thurston	AP	77
Strength	AM	309	Sycamore	GAGL	268	Tavibo	YT	276	Ticonderoga	CV	14
Strickland	DE	333	Sylph	PY	12	Tawakoni	AT	114	Tide	AM	125
Stringham	APD	6	Symbol	AM	123	Tawasa	AT	92	Tiger	GPC	152
Strive	AM	117	Syncline	YO	63	Taylor	DD	468	Tigrone	SS	419
Sturdy	PYc	50	Tackle	ARS	37	Tazha	YT	147	Tilefish	SS	307
Sturgeon	SS	187	Tacoma	PF	3	Teaberry	YN	29	Tillamook	YT	122
Sturtevant	DE	239	Taganak	AO	45	Teak	YN	30	Tillman	DD	641
Suamico	AO	49	Tahchee	YNT	11	Teal	AVP	5	Tills	DE	748
Success	AM	310	Tahoma	GPG	80	Tecumseh	YT	273	Timbalier	AVP	54
Suisun	AVP	53	Takanis Bay	CVE	89	Tekesta	AT	93	Tingey	DD	539
Summit	AMc	106	Takelma	AT	113	Temptress	PG	62	Tinosa	SS	283
Sumner	AGS	5	Talamanca	AF	15	Tenacity	PG	71	Tippecanoe	AO	21
Sumter	APA	52	Talbot	APD	7	Tench	SS	417	Tirante	SS	420
Sundew	GAGL	404	Tallahassee	CL	116	Tenino	AT	115	Tiru	SS	416
Sunfish	SS	281	Tallapoosa	GPG	52	Tennessee	BB	43	Tisdale	DE	33
Sunflower	GAGL	247	Tallulah	AO	50	Tern	AT	142	Titania	AKA	13

Name	Type	No.	Name	Type	No.	Name	Type	No.	Name	Type	No.
Toka	YT	149	Tryon	APH	1	Unimak	AVP	31	Vineyard Sound	GAL	73
Token	AM	126	Tucana	AK	88	Upham	DE	283	Violet	GAGL	250
Toledo	CA	133	Tuckahoe	GYT	89	Upshur	DD	144	Vireo	AT	144
Tolovana	AO	64	Tucker	DD	374	Uranus	AF	14	Virgo	AKA	20
Tolowa	AT	116	Tucson	CL	98	Utah	AG	16	Vixen	PG	53
Tomahawk	AO	88	Tulagi	CVE	72	Ute	AT	76	Vogelgesang	DE	284
Tombigbee	AOG	11	Tularosa	AOG	43	Vagrant	PYc	30	Vulcan	AR	5
Tomich	DE	242	Tulip	GAGL	249	Valcour	AVP	55	W B Preston	AVD	7
Topaz	PYc	10	Tullibee	SS	284	Valiant	PYc	51	W W Burrows	AP	6
Topeka	CL	67	Tulsa	PG	22	Vallejo	CL	112	Wabash	AOG	4
Torchwood	YN	74	Tuluran	AG	46	Valley Forge	CV	37	Wachapreague	AGP	8
Toro	SS	422	Tumult	AM	127	Valor	AMc	108	Wadleigh	DD	689
Torsk	SS	423	Tuna	SS	203	Valve	ARS	28	Wadsworth	DD	516
Totem Bay	CVE	111	Tunny	SS	283	Vamarie	IX	47	Wagner	DE	539
Tourmaline	PY	20	Tupelo	GAGL	303	Van Buren	PF	42	Wahneta	YT	134
Towaliga	AOG	42	Turaco	AMc	55	Van Valkenburgh	DD	656	Wahtah	YT	140
Tracy	DM	19	Turbot	SS	427	Vance	DE	387	Wainwright	DD	419
Transfer	IX	46	Turkey	AT	143	Vandivier	DE	540	Wake Island	CVE	65
Trathen	DD	530	Turner	DD	648	Varian	DE	798	Wakefield	AP	21
Travis	GPC	153	Turquoise	PY	18	Varuna	AGP	5	Wakerobin	GAGL	251
Treasure	YFB	24	Tuscaloosa	CA	37	Vashon	YFB	19	Wakulla	AOG	44
Trembler	SS	424	Tuscana	AKN	3	Vega	AK	17	Waldron	DD	699
Trenton	CL	11	Tuscarora	YT	341	Vela	AK	89	Walke	DD	723
Trepang	SS	412	Tusk	SS	426	Velocity	AM	128	Walker	DD	517
Trever	DMS	16	Tutuila	ARG	4	Vendace	SS	430	Waller	DD	466
Triangulum	AK	102	Tweedy	DE	532	Vent	ARS	29	Walnut	GAGL	252
Trident	AMc	107	Twiggs	DD	591	Venture	PYc	52	Walrus	SS	431
Trigger	SS	237	Twining	DD	540	Vermillion Bay	CVE	108	Walter S Brown	DE	258
Trinity	AO	13	Tyrer	GIX	339	Vernon McNeal	GYP	318	Wampatuck	YT	337
Tripoli	CVE	64	U S Grant	AP	29	Vestal	AR	4	Wandank	AT	26
Trippe	DD	403	Uhlmann	DD	687	Viburnum	YN	76	Wando	YT	123
Triton	GPC	116	Ulua	SS	428	Vicksburg	CL	86	Wapashc.	YNT	13
Triumph	AM	323	Ulvert M Moore	DE	442	Victor	AMc	109	Wapello	YNT	24
Trocadero Bay	CVE	119	Umatilla Reef	CG	6088	Victoria	AO	46	Warbler	ARS	11
Trout	SS	202	Umpqua	AT	25	Vigilance	AM	324	Ward	APD	16
Truant	PYc	14	Unadilla	YT	4	Vigilant	GPC	154	Warren	APA	53
Trumpeter	DE	180	Unalga	GPG	53	Vigor	AMc	110	Warrington	DD	383
Trumpetfish	SS	425	Uncas	YT	242	Viking	ARS	1	Washington	BB	56
Trutta	SS	421	Undaunted	AT	58	Vileehi	IX	62	Wasp	CV	18
Truxton	DE	282	Unicorn	SS	429	Vincennes	CL	64	Wassuc	CMc	3

U. S. NAVAL VESSELS

Name	Type	No.	Name	Type	No.	Name	Type	No.	Name	Type	No.
Wateree	AT	117	Whitehurst	DE	634	Wilmington	CL	111	Wren	DD	568
Waterman	DE	740	Whitewood	YN	84	Wilson	DD	408	Wright	AV	1
Waters	APD	8	Whiting	SS	433	Wimbee	IX	88	Wyffels	DE	6
Watson	DD	482	Whitman	DE	24	Windham Bay	CVE	92	Wyman	DE	38
Watts	DD	567	Whitney	AD	4	Windsor	APA	55	Wyoming	AG	17
Waupaca	AOG	46	Wichita	CA	45	Wingfield	DE	194	Yacona	AOG	45
Wautauga	AOG	22	Wickes	DD	578	Winnebago	GPG	40	Yahara	AOG	37
Waxbill	AMc	15	Widgeon	ASR	1	Winona	GPG	41	Yakutat	AVP	32
Wayne	APA	54	Wileman	DE	22	Winooski	AO	38	Yankton	GYT	72
Weaver	DE	741	Wiley	DD	597	Winslow	DD	359	Yaquima	YT	171
Weber	DE	675	Wilhoite	DE	397	Winter Quarter	GAL	107	Yarnall	DD	541
Wedderburn	DD	684	Wilkes	DD	441	Winterberry	YN	75	Yaupon	YN	96
Weeden	DE	797	Wilkes Barre	CL	103	Wintle	DE	25	Yeaton	GPC	156
Weehawken	CM	12	Will P Biddle	APA	8	Wisconsin	BB	64	Yew	YN	32
Weeks	DE	285	Willapa Bay	CVE	109	Wiseman	DE	667	Yokes	DE	668
Weight	ARS	35	Willet	ARS	12	Wistaria	GAGL	254	Yonaguska	YT	195
Welles	DD	628	William C Cole	DE	286	Witter	DE	636	Yorktown	CV	10
Wenatchee	AT	118	William C Miller	DE	259	Woban	YT	138	Yosemite	AD	19
Wenonah	YT	148	William D Porter	DD	579	Wolffish	SS	434	Young	DD	580
Wesson	DE	184	William M Hobby	DE	236	Wolverine	IX	64	Youngstown	CL	94
West Point	AP	23	William M Wood	DE	287	Woodbine	GAGL	289	Yukon	AF	9
West Virginia	BB	48	William R Rush	DE	288	Woodbury	GPC	155	Yuma	AT	94
Westwind	GPG	281	William Seiverling	DE	441	Woodcliff Bay	CVE	93	Zaca	IX	73
Whale	SS	239	William T Powell	DE	213	Woodcock	AT	145	Zane	DMS	14
Wharton	AP	7	Williams	DE	290	Woodrush	GAGL	407	Zaniah	AK	120
Whippet	IX	129	Williamsburg	PG	56	Woodworth	DD	460	Zaurak	AK	117
Whipple	DD	217	Williamson	DD	244	Woolsey	DD	437	Zeal	AM	131
Whippoorwill	AM	35	Willis	DE	395	Woonsocket	PF	32	Zebra	IX	107
Whipstock	YO	49	Willmarth	DE	638	Worcester	PF	62	Zeilin	APA	3
White Marsh	LSD	8	Willoughby	AGP	9	Worden	DD	352	Zinnia	GAGL	255
White Plains	CVE	66	Willow	GAGL	253	Woyot	YT	150	Zircon	PY	16
Whitefish	SS	432	Wilmette	IX	29	Wrangell	AE	12	Zuni	AT	95

U. S. BATTLESHIPS

U. S. BATTLESHIPS

SOUTH DAKOTA Class
57 SOUTH DAKOTA
58 INDIANA
59 MASSACHUSETTS
60 ALABAMA

TENNESSEE Class
43 TENNESSEE
44 CALIFORNIA
(WEST VIRGINIA similar)

NEW MEXICO Class
40 NEW MEXICO
41 MISSISSIPPI
42 IDAHO
38 PENNSYLVANIA
36 NEVADA

NEW YORK Class
35 TEXAS
34 NEW YORK
33 ARKANSAS

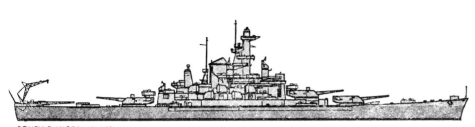

SOUTH DAKOTA CLASS

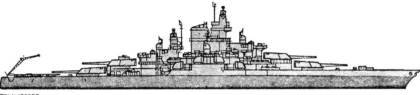

TENNESSEE

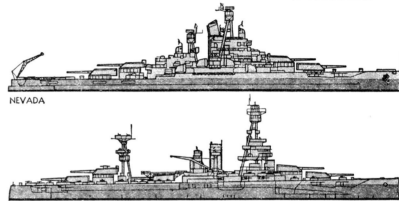

NEVADA

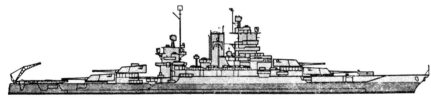

NEW MEXICO CLASS

NEW YORK CLASS

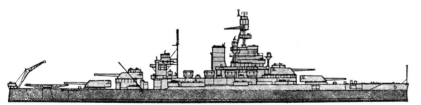

PENNSYLVANIA

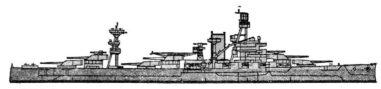

ARKANSAS

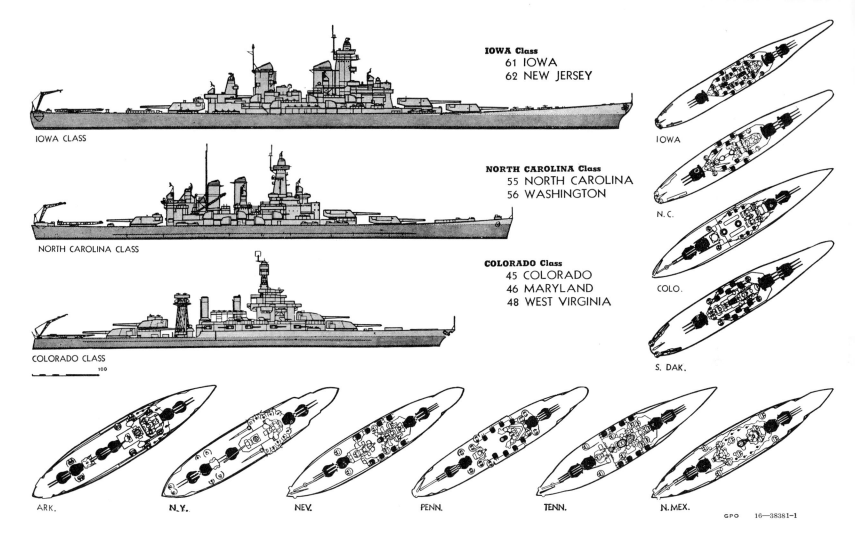

IOWA Class
61 IOWA
62 NEW JERSEY

IOWA CLASS

NORTH CAROLINA Class
55 NORTH CAROLINA
56 WASHINGTON

NORTH CAROLINA CLASS

COLORADO Class
45 COLORADO
46 MARYLAND
48 WEST VIRGINIA

COLORADO CLASS

100

IOWA

N. C.

COLO.

S. DAK.

ARK. N.Y. NEV. PENN. TENN. N. MEX.

GPO   16—38381-1

IOWA Class (BB)

Bow —36'
Stern —22'
Bridge —65'
Stack —98'
Mast —134'

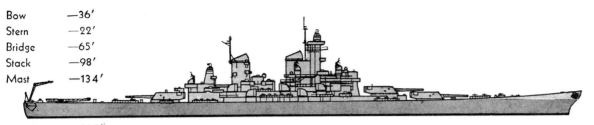

Length o. a. —887'

Ships in Class:

IOWA	—BB 61
NEW JERSEY	—BB 62
MISSOURI	—BB 63
WISCONSIN	—BB 64

Observer's note:

—Flush hull, tower foremast, wide stacks, and hull lines follow same basic design as appears in all new combatant types.

—Easily confused with NORTH CAROLINA class at distances.

▼ IOWA—photo 4-4-43.

IOWA Class (BB)

Plan view of IOWA illustrates enlarged SOUTH DAKOTA—NORTH CAROLINA design in island and armament arrangement. Distinctive tapered bow and stern differentiate this from all other ships.

Photos of the NEW JERSEY, 7-8-43 and 8-5-43.

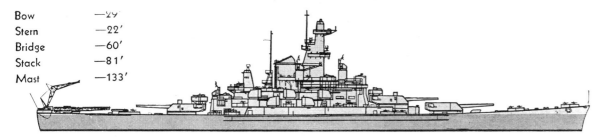

Bow —29'
Stern —22'
Bridge —60'
Stack —81'
Mast —133'

Length o. a.—680'

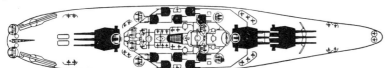

SOUTH DAKOTA Class (BB)

Ships in Class:

SOUTH DAKOTA—BB 57
INDIANA   —BB 58
MASSACHUSETTS—BB 59
ALABAMA   —BB 60

All were commissioned in 1942.

Observer's note:

—Combined tower bridge and broad stack, designed to confuse bearing and add greater AA arc of fire.
—Flush, broad hull, island arrangement, and main battery disposition (2–A–1) similar to NORTH CAROLINA and IOWA.

Photo of SOUTH DAKOTA below illustrates secondary battery arrangement and bow 40 mm, distinctive of this ship. ▼

SOUTH DAKOTA Class (BB)

▲▼ All photos are of the ALABAMA, taken 2-43, 8-43. Note prominent slit in hull below main deck and pyramidal superstructure.

SOUTH DAKOTA Class (BB)

▲ Units of the SOUTH DAKOTA and KING GEORGE V classes.　　▼ ALABAMA　　▲ SOUTH DAKOTA, photo 7-22-42, shows boats and cranes, since removed.

NORTH CAROLINA Class (BB)

NORTH CAROLINA Class (BB)

Ships in Class:

NORTH CAROLINA—BB 55
WASHINGTON —BB 56

Observer's note:

—Flush hull, tower bridge, two large vertical stacks

—2–A–1 main battery disposition (triples).

—Distinquishing feature is distance between stacks and tower bridge.

Photo below is of WASHINGTON, 11/12/43, other page of NORTH CAROLINA—quartering views (1942) show boats and handling cranes, since removed.

Bow	—31'
Stern	—20'
Bridge	—62'
Stack	—88'
Mast	—122'

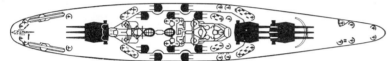

Length o. a. —740'6"

COLORADO Class (BB)

▼ COLORADO—photo 11-8-42.   ▲ MARYLAND, photographed in Pacific camouflage on 11-12-43. ▼   TENNESSEE is in the background.

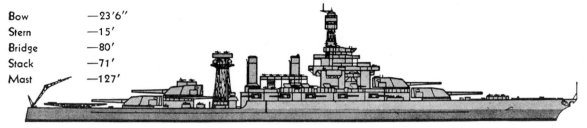

Bow — 23'6"
Stern — 15'
Bridge — 80'
Stack — 71'
Mast — 127'

Length o. a. —624'

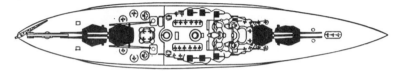

COLORADO Class (BB)

Ships in Class:

COLORADO — BB 45
MARYLAND — BB 46
WEST VIRGINIA — BB 48

WEST VIRGINIA is undergoing reconstruction similar to the TENNESSEE Class.

Observer's note:
— Cage masts, two thin S. P. stacks.
— Same hull as NEW MEXICO class— broken amidships.
— 2-A-2 (twins) main battery arrangement.

MARYLAND, photo 11-8-42. Shows single DP shields and secondary casemate battery—typical of this class. ▼

TENNESSEE Class (BB)

▼ These photos, taken 5–43, illustrate two distinctive features of this ship—the tremendous beam resulting from an added blister, and the stepped DP battery arrangement.   ▲ 1–11–44

TENNESSEE Class (BB)

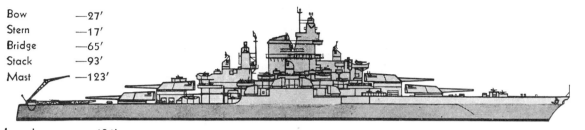

Bow —27'
Stern —17'
Bridge —65'
Stack —93'
Mast —123'

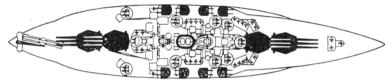

Length o. a. —624'

Ships in Class:

TENNESSEE —BB 43
CALIFORNIA—BB 44

CALIFORNIA and WEST VIRGINIA are undergoing similar wartime modernization.

Observer's note:

—Tower foremast faired into large capped stack. Tower mainmast with stepped pole.

—2-A-2 main battery arrangement (like NEW MEXICO).

—Easily mistaken for SOUTH DAKOTA class or Germany's TIRPITZ.

NEW MEXICO Class (BB)

▼ NEW MEXICO—12-4-43   ▲ MISSISSIPPI—10-8-43 ▲

NEW MEXICO Class (BB)

Ships in Class:
NEW MEXICO—BB 40
MISSISSIPPI —BB 41
IDAHO —BB 42

Observer's note:

—High upright stack abaft heavy tower bridge. (Stack cap to be added.)

—Clipper bow, cruiser stern, hull broken amidships.

—20 mm. platform variation differentiate IDAHO (drawing) from other units.

Main armament similar to TENNESSEE class.

▼ NEW MEXICO, photo 1942.

Bow —24'
Stern —15'
Bridge —95'
Stack —83'
Mast —118'

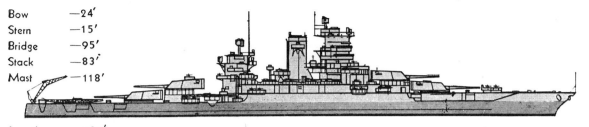

Length o. a.— 624'

PENNSYLVANIA. (BB)

PENNSYLVANIA (BB 38)

Bow —26'
Stern —15'
Bridge —76'
Stack —76'
Mast —127'

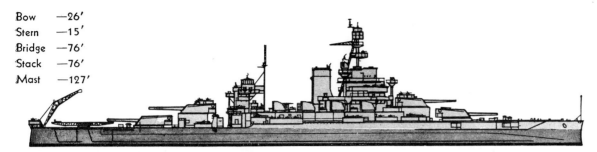

Length o. a.—600'

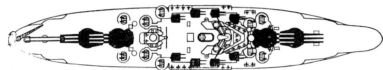

Observer's note:

—Tripod foremast, heavy bridge, single stack.

—Broken hull outline, rounded bow and stern, and DP battery arrangement distinguish this ship from the air.

—2 A-2 (triples) main battery arrangement.

—Resembles British ROYAL SOVEREIGN, Japan's NAGATO battleship classes.

Photos—1943.

NEVADA (BB)

All photos taken 9–2–43, 12–14–42, and 7–14–43.

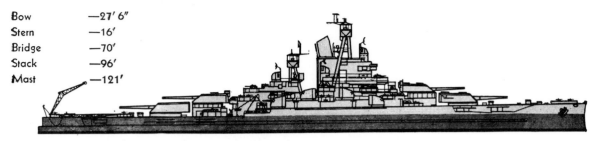

Bow —27' 6"
Stern —16'
Bridge —70'
Stack —96'
Mast —121'

Length o. a. —575'

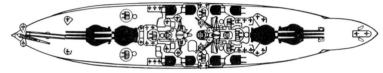

Observer's note:

—Low bridge, tripod foremast, large stack, and stump tripod mainmast; all are consolidated into an integrated island arrangement.

—Distinctive feature is raked stack extension.

—2–A–2 main battery disposition (twins over triples) and hull shape differentiates this from other old BB's.

NEW YORK Class (BB)

▲ Photos of TEXAS show catapult and boat cranes amidships, both distinctive features of this class. Photos 3–15–42.

▲ NEW YORK, 1942.

NEW YORK Class (BB)

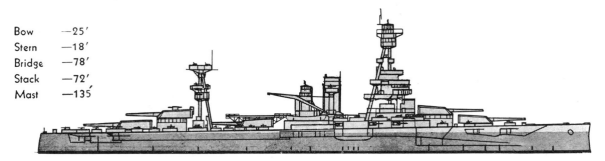

Bow   —25'
Stern   —18'
Bridge —78'
Stack   —72'
Mast   —135'

Length o. a. —573'

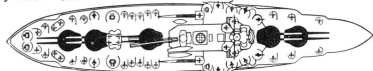

Ships in Class:
  NEW YORK—BB 34
  TEXAS   —BB 35

Observer's note:

—Two tripod masts, tall single stack flanked
  by large boat cranes.

—Typical OBB flush hull.

--2–A–1–2 main battery arrangement.

—Like other older U. S. BB's, this class resembles many of the British and Japanese
  battleship classes.

TEXAS, photo 3–15–43.   Note 5" case-
mates and heavy AAMG armament. ▼

ARKANSAS
7-1-43 ▲
6-27-42 ▼

Bow   —27'
Stern   —20'
Bridge   —59'
Stack   —72'
Mast   —103'

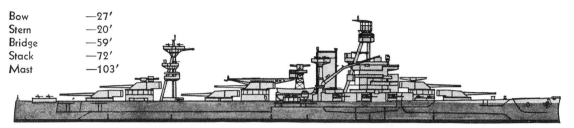

Length o. a.   —554'

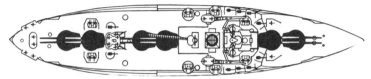

1-2-43 ▼

Ships in Class:
  ARKANSAS —BB 40
  WYOMING—AG 17

WYOMING (silhouette), partially demilitarized, serves as a Gunnery Training Ship.

Observer's note:

—2–A–2–2 main battery disposition (Japan's ISE Class similar).

—Low, widely spaced tripod masts (WYOMING retains original cage foremast).

—Catapult on No. 3 turret, single stack flanked by prominent cranes.

The distance shots of the battleships illustrated are included as an aid in their identification. The top row shows units of the NEW MEXICO, COLORADO, TENNESSEE, and PENNSYLVANIA Classes, all photos taken during recent operations. The bottom row illustrates ships of the SOUTH DAKOTA, NEW YORK, and NORTH CAROLINA Classes.

U. S. CARRIERS

U. S. CARRIERS

CV

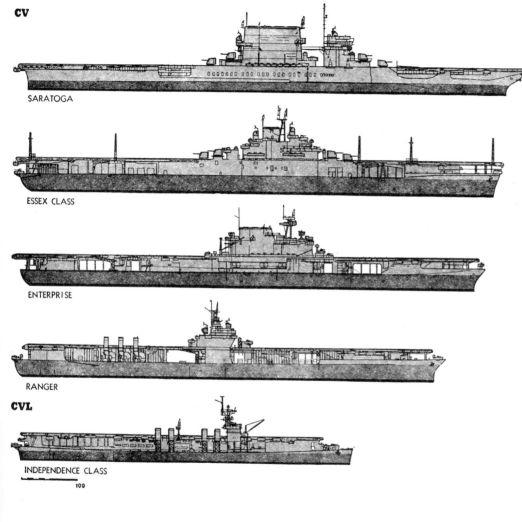

SARATOGA

ESSEX CLASS

ENTERPRISE

RANGER

CVL

INDEPENDENCE CLASS

100

AIRCRAFT CARRIERS (CV)

CV 3 SARATOGA
CV 4 RANGER
CV 6 ENTERPRISE

Essex Class:

CV 9 ESSEX
CV 10 YORKTOWN
CV 11 INTREPID
CV 12 HORNET
CV 13 FRANKLIN
CV 14 TICONDEROGA
CV 15 RANDOLPH
CV 16 LEXINGTON
CV 17 BUNKER HILL
CV 18 WASP
CV 19 HANCOCK
CV 20 BENNINGTON

AIRCRAFT CARRIERS, CRUISER HULL (CVL)
Independence Class:

22 INDEPENDENCE
23 PRINCETON
24 BELLEAU WOOD
25 COWPENS
26 MONTEREY
27 LANGLEY
28 CABOT
29 BATAAN
30 SAN JACINTO

LONG ISLAND

CHARGER

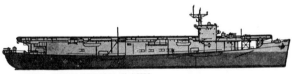

BOGUE—PRINCE WILLIAM CLASSES

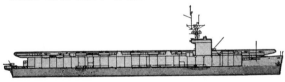

CASABLANCA CLASS

SANGAMON CLASS

AUXILIARY AIRCRAFT CARRIERS (CVE)

CVE 1 LONG ISLAND
CVE 30 CHARGER

Bogue-Prince William Class:

CVE 9 BOGUE
CVE 11 CARD
CVE 12 COPAHEE
CVE 13 CORE
CVE 16 NASSAU
CVE 18 ALTAMAHA
CVE 20 BARNES
CVE 21 BLOCK ISLAND
CVE 23 BRETON
CVE 25 CROATAN
CVE 31 PRINCE WILLIAM

Sangamon Class:

CVE 26 SANGAMON
CVE 27 SUWANEE
CVE 28 CHENANGO
CVE 29 SANTEE

AUXILIARY AIRCRAFT CARRIERS (CVE)

Casablanca Class

CVE 55 CASABLANCA	CVE 73 GAMBLER BAY	CVE 90 THETIS BAY
CVE 57 CORAL SEA	CVE 74 NEHENTA BAY	CVE 91 ULITAKA BAY
CVE 58 CORREGIDOR	CVE 75 HOGGATT BAY	CVE 92 WINDHAM BAY
CVE 59 MISSION BAY	CVE 76 KABASHAN BAY	CVE 93 WOODCLIFF
CVE 60 GUADALCANAL	CVE 77 KANALKU BAY	CVE 94 ALAZON BAY
CVE 61 MANILA BAY	CVE 78 KAITA BAY	CVE 95 ALIKULA BAY
CVE 62 NATOMA BAY	CVE 79 OMMANEY BAY	CVE 96 ANGUILLA
CVE 63 MIDWAY	CVE 80 PETROF BAY	CVE 97 ASTROLABE BAY
CVE 64 TRIPOLI	CVE 81 RUDYERD BAY	CVE 98 BUCARELI BAY
CVE 65 WAKE ISLAND	CVE 82 SAGINAW BAY	CVE 99 CHAPIN BAY
CVE 66 WHITE PLAINS	CVE 83 SARGENT BAY	CVE 100 DIDRICKSON BAY
CVE 67 NASSUK BAY	CVE 84 SHAMBROCK BAY	CVE 101 DOLOMI BAY
CVE 68 KALININ BAY	CVE 85 SHIPLEY BAY	CVE 102 ATTU
CVE 69 KASAAN BAY	CVE 86 SITKOH BAY	CVE 103 ALAVA BAY
CVE 70 FANSHAW	CVE 87 STEAMER BAY	CVE 104 MUNDA
CVE 71 KITKUN BAY	CVE 88 TANANEK BAY	CVE 105 ST. JOSEPH
CVE 72 FORTAZELA BAY	CVE 89 TAKANIS BAY	CVE 106 SUNSET

Deck   —57'
Bridge   —93'
Stack   —113'
Mast   —147'

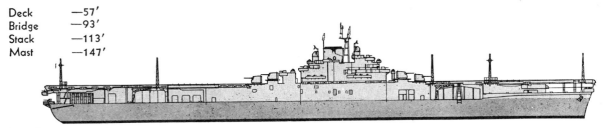

Length o. a. —885'

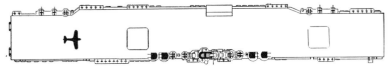

Ships in Class:

ESSEX	—CV 9	RANDOLPH	—CV 15
YORKTOWN	—10	LEXINGTON	—16
INTREPID	—11	BUNKER HILL	—17
HORNET	—12	WASP	—18
FRANKLIN	—13	HANCOCK	—19
TICONDEROGA	—14	BENNINGTON	—20

Observer's Note:

—Long, pyramidal superstructure.
—Small stack, tripod mast.
—Notice freeboard is relatively unbroken.
—Rectangular, full-length flight deck.

▼ ESSEX (5-10-43) carrying TBF's and SBD's.

ESSEX Class (CV)

▲ Photos show LEXINGTON—3-29-43. Port elevator is shown flush with deck in broadside, secured upright in aerial of BUNKER HILL ▼ Photo 5-24-43. The tall radio masts are distinctive of this class and British carriers.

▲ A Task Force, including BUNKER HILL, ESSEX, and NORTH CAROLINA. Note resemblance to ILLUSTRIOUS class (BRITISH CV). Photo 11–12–43

▼ ESSEX, CV 9. Starboard radio masts here swung outboard. Planes carried are SBD's and F6F's.

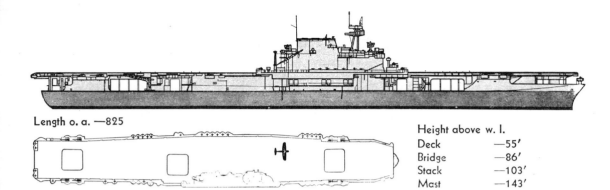

Length o. a. —825

Height above w. l.

Deck —55'
Bridge —86'
Stack —103'
Mast —143'

Observer's Note:

—Long, high island superstructure combined with heavy stack.

—Short tripod foremast with stick mainmast stepped abaft stack.

—Full-length flight deck, broken freeboard.

▼ Photo below dated 6–7–43, on opposite page, 11–10–42

▼ Photo, taken 10–21–43, shows recent minor alterations.

RANGER (CV)

Photos taken 1-6-43. Notice the numerous AAMG positions and open 5-inch gun mounts flanking the flight deck. Also prominent in these views is the characteristic broken freeboard

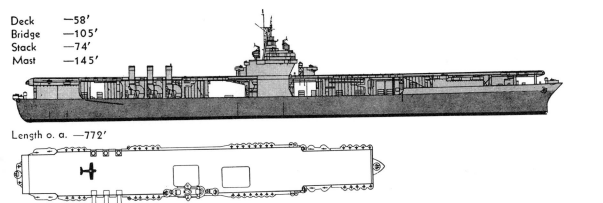

Deck — 58'
Bridge — 105'
Stack — 74'
Mast — 145'

Length o. a. — 772'

Observer's note:

—Small pyramidal island superstructure.

—Freeboard broken for full length of ship.

—Symmetrical flight deck, short of full length at both bow and stern.

—Six stacks, port and starboard, swing outboard when aircraft are operated.

Notice amidships elevators, usually fore and aft on most carriers.

SARATOGA (CV)

▲ Photos 11-6-42 showing new 20 and 40 MM machine gun positions, and other minor superstructural alterations. ▼

SARATOGA—CV 3

Deck   —45'
Bridge   —95'
Stack   —110'
Mast   —155'

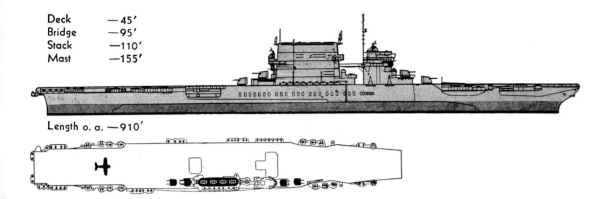

Length o. a. —910'

Observer's note:

—100' encased stack, separate bridge.

—Only U. S. carrier with integral hull and flight deck, a feature common with the British ILLUSTRIOUS class.

—Original 8'' turrets replaced by 5'' twins. Large deck-level platforms support rows of 5'' singles, 40 mm. quads, and 20 mm. mounts.

—This is the longest warship afloat.

▼ Photo 11-12-42

INDEPENDENCE Class (CVL)

▲ COWPENS and PRINCETON   ▼—Deck extended between stacks and quad mounts on bow and stern are recent changes.

INDEMENDENCE CLASS—CVL

Deck —46'
Bridge —68'
Stack —58'
Mast —117'

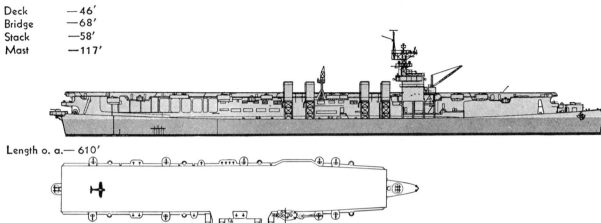

Length o. a.— 610'

Converted from CL (CLEVELAND Class) hulls as an emergency measure, these ships are a unique design not found in other navies. The short flight deck is limited by the fine lines of the cruiser hull.

Observer's note:

—4 prominent square starboard stacks (hinged).

—CVE box bridge and trestle mast.

—Enclosed freeboard up to flight-deck.

—May be mistaken for CVE's.

▼ CVL 23—PRINCETON 5-31-43.   Note transom stern.

▼ CVL 25—COWPENS 7-17-43.   Planes carried are F6S's TBF's, and SBD's.

INDEPENDENCE Class (CVL)

▲ Note general CVE appearance at distances.

▲ CVL 22—INDEPENDENCE.

▼ CVL 26—MONTEREY, photographed 7–17–43, with two SNJ's on the flight deck. This is the only Carrier class equipped with the crane and stump radio masts illustrated.

CHARGER—CVE 30

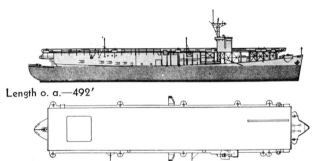

Observer's Note:
—Freighter hull, enclosed to flight deck aft, open forward.
—Trestle mast on LONG ISLAND tops box bridge on CHARGER.
—Note CHARGER is the only CVE without a raised forecastle.

Length o. a.—492'

Height above w. l. Bridge—69' Deck—52' Mast—88'

LONG ISLAND—CVE 1

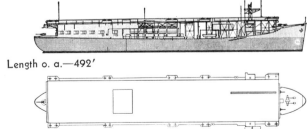

Length o. a.—492'

Height above w. l. Deck—58' Mast—69'

▲ USS BARNES, photographed 7-1-43, while ferrying a load of Thunderbolts and dismantled Lightnings.

CROATAN photographed 5-20-43. ▼

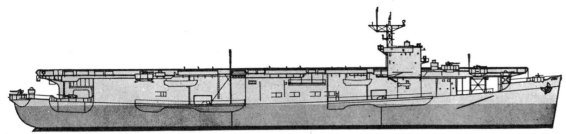

Length o. a. —494'

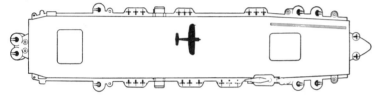

Height above w. l.
Bridge   —73'
Deck   —54'
Mast   —90'

Although divided into two classes there are no apparent appearance variations.

Observer's Note:
—Hull enclosed to flight deck.
—Standard CVE box bridge topped by trestle mast.
—Distinguished from other classes by presence of hull sponsons.
—Sisterships form British BATTLER class.

6-24-42 ▼

SANTEE Class—CVE

▼ SANGAMON, 9-11-42. Note TBF's, SBD's on flight deck. Below is SANTEE as camouflaged 9-42.

SANGAMON Class—CVE

Height above w. l.

Bridge —59'

Deck —42'

Mast —84', 108'

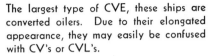

The largest type of CVE, these ships are converted oilers. Due to their elongated appearance, they may easily be confused with CV's or CVL's.

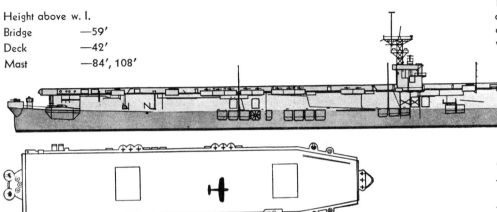

Observer's Note:

—Hull enclosed to flight deck, with numerous rectangular openings in freeboard.

—Standard CVE box bridge and trestle mast.

Length o. a.—553'

9-19-42

▼ SANTEE   10-12-43

CASABLANCA CLASS—CVE

Additional views of the CORAL SEA show the four small exhausts amidships and the symmetrical armament disposition, distinctive of this class.

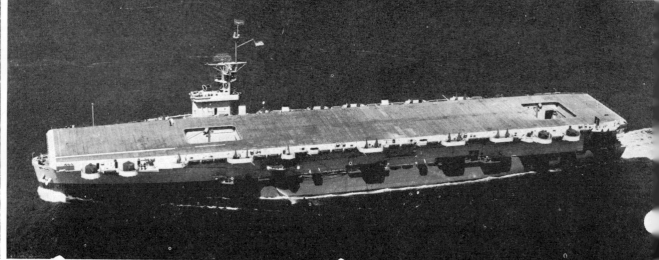

CASABLANCA Class—CVE

Deck   —41'
Bridge   —60'
Mast   —113'

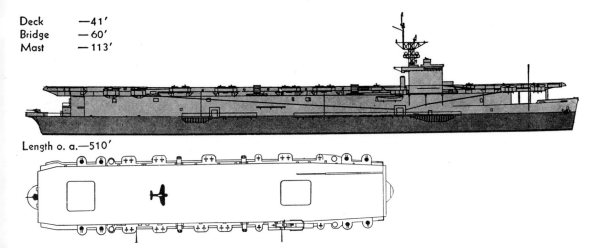

Length o. a.—510'

Shorter than converted types, the flight deck of this design is, however, much broader (80'). The small hull limits the AA battery to deck positions.

Observer's Note:

—Distinguished from other CVE's by trim hull lines and broad transom stern.
—Rectangular flight deck and small hull sponsons similar to Bogue Class.

—Freeboard relatively unbroken.

All Photos of CVE 57—CORAL SEA.

BRITISH (LEND LEASE) CVE

The bulk of the British escort carrier fleet is made up of sister ships of classes previously illustrated. Only minor differences serve to distinguish them from our ships. All types are illustrated in ONI-201, Warships of the British Commonwealth.

▲ ARCHER, a sister ship of the LONG ISLAND, and BITER (right), similar to CHARGER—are units of the ARCHER Class.
▼ STRIKER, one of the BATTLER Class, is of the same design as our BOGUE-PRINCE WILLIAM Class. Of the latter class, all units but Prince William are operating with the Br...

U. S. CRUISERS

HEAVY CRUISERS

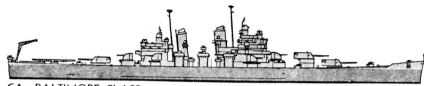

CA—BALTIMORE CLASS

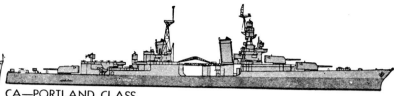

CA—PORTLAND CLASS

CA—WICHITA

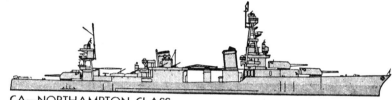

CA—NORTHAMPTON CLASS

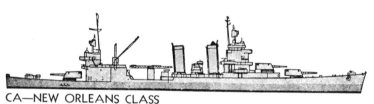

CA—NEW ORLEANS CLASS

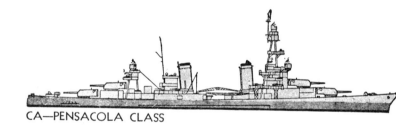

CA—PENSACOLA CLASS

BALTIMORE Class

68 BALTIMORE
69 BOSTON
70 CANBERRA
71 QUINCY
72 PITTSBURG
73 ST. PAUL

45 WICHITA

NEW ORLEANS Class

32 NEW ORLEANS
36 MINNEAPOLIS
37 TUSCALOOSA
38 SAN FRANCISCO

PORTLAND Class

33 PORTLAND
35 INDIANAPOLIS

NORTHAMPTON Class

27 CHESTER
28 LOUISVILLE
31 AUGUSTA

PENSACOLA Class

24 PENSACOLA
25 SALT LAKE CITY

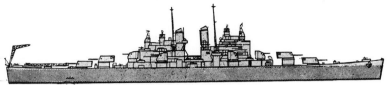

CL—CLEVELAND-VINCENNES CLASS

CL—BROOKLYN-PHOENIX CLASS

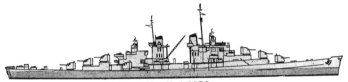

CL—ATLANTA-OAKLAND CLASSES

CL—ST. LOUIS

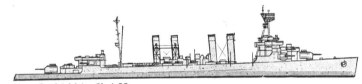

CL—OMAHA CLASS

ATLANTA-OAKLAND Class
- 53 SAN DIEGO
- 54 SAN JUAN
- 95 OAKLAND
- 96 RENO
- 97 FLINT
- 98 TUCSON

CLEVELAND-VINCENNES Class
- 55 CLEVELAND
- 56 COLUMBIA
- 57 MONTPELIER
- 58 DENVER
- 60 SANTA FE
- 62 BIRMINGHAM
- 63 MOBILE
- 64 VINCENNES
- 65 PASADENA
- 66 SPRINGFIELD
- 67 TOPEKA
- 80 BILOXI
- 81 HOUSTON
- 86 VICKBURG
- 87 DULUTH
- 89 MIAMI
- 90 ASTORIA

BROOKLYN-PHOENIX Class
- 40 BROOKLYN
- 41 PHILADELPHIA
- 42 SAVANNAH
- 43 NASHVILLE
- 46 PHOENIX
- 47 BOISE
- 48 HONOLULU

- 49 ST. LOUIS

OMAHA Class
- 4 OMAHA
- 5 MILWAUKEE
- 6 CINCINNATI
- 7 RALEIGH
- 8 DETROIT
- 9 RICHMOND
- 10 CONCORD
- 11 TRENTON
- 12 MARBLEHEAD
- 13 MEMPHIS

BALTIMORE Class (CA)

Bow —33'
Stern —25'
Bridge —71'
Stack —86'
Mast —112'

Length o. a. — 673'

BALTIMORE Class—CA

Ships in Class:
BALTIMORE —CA 68
BOSTON —CA 69
CANBERRA —CA 70
QUINCY —CA 71
PITTSBURG —CA 72
ST. PAUL —CA 73

Observer's note:
—Like other newer cruisers, has flush hull, transom stern, two raking stacks, and pole masts.
—2–A–1 main battery arrangement with centerline DP mounts (like WICHITA).

Ships illustrated are the BALTIMORE and BOSTON.

BALTIMORE Class—CA

Photos of CA 68, BALTIMORE, dated 7–9–43, show distinctive secondary battery arrangement. Planes are OS2U—KINGFISHERS.

Bow —30'
Stern —25'
Bridge —58'
Stack —73'
Mast —113'

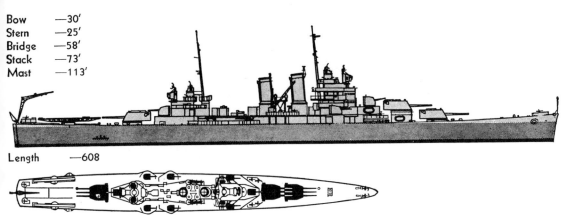

Length —608

Observer's note:

—Flush hull, wide transom stern.

—Two closely spaced, raking stacks, pole masts.

—2–A–1 main battery arrangement; note superimposed secondaries.

—Note marked similarity to BROOKLYN-PHOENIX units, particularly at a distance.

—May be mistaken for the German KÖLN class CL's or EMDEN.

Recent changes are shown in the photos, dated 11–18–43.

NEW ORLEANS Class (CA)

▲ SAN FRANCISCO, 2-15-43, and NEW ORLEANS, ▼ 7-30-43

Two other units shown recovering their SOC's.

Recent alterations—
—Bridge reduced and conning tower removed for increased stability.
—Starboard plane-handling crane removed.
—Amidships searchlight platform reduced.
—AA positions added.
Photo below shows pre-modernization appearance.

NEW ORLEANS Class—CA

Bow —29'
Stern —16'
Bridge —77'
Stack —75'
Mast 116'

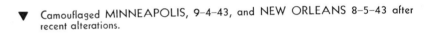

Length o. a.—580'

Ships in class:

NEW ORLEANS —CA 32
MINNEAPOLIS —CA 36
TUSCALOOSA —CA 37
SAN FRANCISCO—CA 38

Observer's note:

—Two closely spaced, heavy, raked stacks.

—Amidships catapults and large hangar aft.

—2–A–1 main battery disposition.

—Resembles German KÖLN class and EMDEN, light cruisers.

▼ Camouflaged MINNEAPOLIS, 9-4-43, and NEW ORLEANS 8-5-43 after recent alterations.

Photos show
both PORTLAND and
INDIANAPOLIS, 5–43.

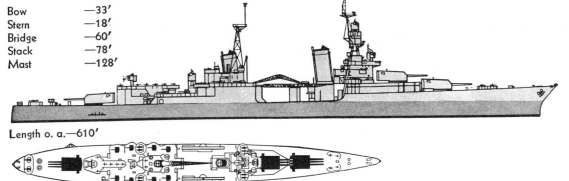

Bow —33'
Stern —18'
Bridge —60'
Stack —78'
Mast —128'

Length o. a.—610'

PORTLAND Class—CA 33, 35

Ships in Class:

PORTLAND —CA 33
INDIANAPOLIS—CA 35

Recent changes brought about by the need for increased stability and anti-aircraft armament have radically changed the appearance of these ships.

Observer's note:

—Cruiser hull, deck line broken amidships.

—Two raked, flat sided stacks, separated by catapult well deck.

—Heavy, low tripod foremast, light tripod mainmast at No. 2 stack.

Classed separately, the AUGUSTA differs in position of hull break and minor superstructure details.

AUGUSTA, 1-29-44 ▶

▼ Camouflaged LOUISVILLE and CHESTER

Bow —33'
Stern —20'
Bridge —66'
Stack —76'
Mast —138'

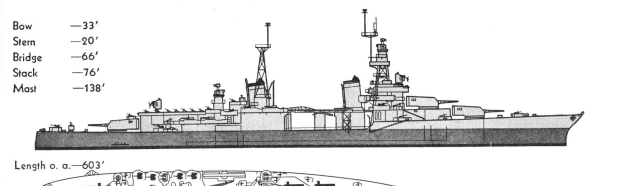

Length o. a.—603'

Ships in Class:
  CHESTER   —CA 27
  LOUISVILLE—CA 28
  AUGUSTA   —CA 31

Current armament and superstructure changes are indicated in the drawing.

Observer's note:

—Cruiser hull, deck line broken at catapult in AUGUSTA, at foremast in other units.

—Tall tripod foremast, light tripod main-mast encircling No. 2 stack (authorized).

—Two short raking, combined stacks.

PENSACOLA Class—CA

All Photos are of SALT LAKE CITY, 5–10–43.

PENSACOLA Class—CA 24, 25

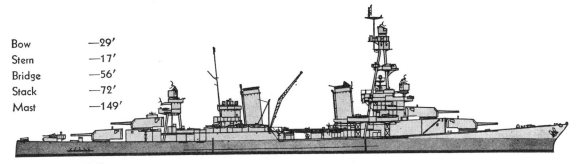

Bow — 29'
Stern — 17'
Bridge — 56'
Stack — 72'
Mast — 149'

Length o. a. — 585'

Ships in Class:
  PENSACOLA   —CA 24
  SALT LAKE CITY—CA 25

These ships are scheduled for changes simi-lar to the PORTLAND.

Observer's note:

—2–A–2 main battery disposition (triples over twins).

—Tall tripod foremast, pole mainmast, plus a tripod control tower aft.

—Two heavy, widely separated raking stacks.

—Flush hull, catapults amidships.

San Juan, 6-3-43. ▼ ▲ Oakland, 8-2-43. ▶

▼ Oakland, 8-2-43. ▼

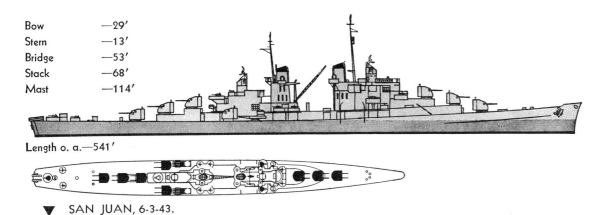

Bow	—29'
Stern	—13'
Bridge	—53'
Stack	—68'
Mast	—114'

Length o. a.—541'

▼ SAN JUAN, 6-3-43.

Ship in Class:
SAN DIEGO —CL 53
SAN JUAN —CL 54
OAKLAND —CL 95
RENO —CL 96
Sister ships are building.

Observer's note:
—Flush hull with pronounced sheer forward.
—3–A–3 main battery arrangement.
(Note: OAKLAND has no wing mounts.)
—Two thin stacks combined with super-structure.
—ATLANTA'S secondary armament is to be altered to conform with OAKLAND.

OAKLAND, 8-2-43. ▼

CLEVELAND-VINCENNES Class (CL)

CLEVELAND-VINCENNES Class—CL

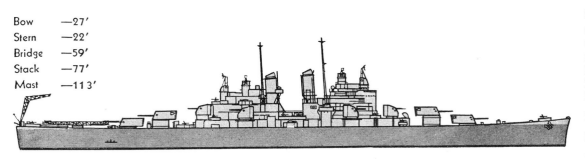

Bow —27'
Stern —22'
Bridge —59'
Stack —77'
Mast —113'

Length o. a.—610'

Ships in Class.

CLEVELAND	—CL 55	SPRINGFIELD	—CL 66
COLUMBIA	—CL 56	TOPEKA	—CL 67
MONTPELIER	—CL 57	BILOXI	—CL 80
DENVER	—CL 58	HOUSTON	—CL 81
SANTA FE	—CL 60	VICKSBURG	—CL 86
BIRMINGHAM	—CL 62	DULUTH	—CL 87
MOBILE	—CL 63	MIAMI	—CL 89
VINCENNES	—CL 64	ASTORIA	—CL 90
PASADENA	—CL 65		

Observer's note:

—Flush hull, two thin stacks, pole masts.

—2–A–2 main battery disposition (triples).

—Note symmetrical profile.

Photo below of CL 63—MOBILE, dated 5-2-43—on opposite page CL 62—BIRMINGHAM, 2-20-43.

CLEVELAND-VINCENNES Class—CL

Broadside shows CL 80, BILOXI, a unit of the new Vincennes group. Compare slight super-structure and AA armament variations with CL 58, DENVER (Cleveland group) shown below.

Bow   —29'
Stern   —21'
Bridge   —53'
Stack   —72'
Mast   —128'

Length o. a.—608'

Completed in 1939 as the last of the BROOKLYN class.

Observer's note:

—Differs from BROOKLYN in location of mainmast and superstructure close abaft second stack.

—Secondary battery in twin turrets. BROOKLYN's have single mounts.

Cut-down bridge and searchlight platform, additional AA positions are recent changes — Photos, 10–16–43.

BROOKLYN-PHOENIX Class (CL)

BOISE ► SAVANNAH ▲

BOISE ► HONOLULU ▲

PHILADELPHIA ► PHOENIX ▲

BROOKLYN-PHOENIX Class—CL

Bow   —27'
Stern   —23'
Bridge   —52'
Stack   —67
Mast   —116'

Length o. a.—608'

Ships in Class:

BROOKLYN	—CL 40
PHILADELPHIA	—CL 41
SAVANNAH	—CL 42
NASHVILLE	—CL 43
PHOENIX	—CL 46
BOISE	—CL 47
HONOLULU	—CL 48

Observer's note:

—Flush hull, transom stern, two closely spaced raking stacks, pole masts.

—2-1-A-2 main battery arrangement (similar to Jap CA's).

▼ PHOENIX, photo 9-23-43, shows latest superstructure changes.

OMAHA Class (CL)

▲ TRENTON and CONCORD ▼ show distinctive broken deckline and tapered stern.   Note that the main battery is disposed in centerline and casemated mounts.

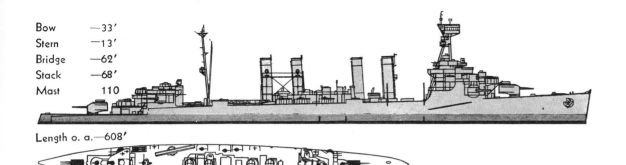

Bow —33'
Stern —13'
Bridge —62'
Stack —68'
Mast 110

Length o. a.—608'

Ships in Class:

OMAHA —CL 4
MILWAUKEE —CL 5
CINCINNATI —CL 6
RALEIGH —CL 7
DETROIT —CL 8
RICHMOND —CL 9
CONCORD —CL 10
TRENTON —CL 11
MARBLEHEAD —CL 12
MEMPHIS —CL 13

Observer's note:

—With Jap SENDAI, constitute the only operational 4-stackers larger than destroyers.

—Minor superstructure variations occur among units.

▼ CL 11—TRENTON, photo 5–11–43.

▲ Group shot of DDs, BBs, APD, and LSTs was taken over Adak harbor.
Distance views show CLEVELAND, BROOKLYN, and NEW ORLEANS units below, NORTHAMPTON and PENSACOLA above.

U. S. DESTROYERS

DESTROYERS

All U. S. Destroyer classes are silhouetted below. For recognition purposes some may be combined in groups as follows: Sumner–Fletcher, Livermore–Benson, Benham–Sims–Gridley–Bagley (small one-stackers), Mahan–Porter, and old "Flush Deckers" (DD–DM–DMS–AVD–APD).

Since destroyers of all navies are similar in appearance, it is important to learn their class resemblances. Fletcher class closely resembles the German Narviks, Japanese Fubukis; Livermores and Mahans at a distance are similar to all Japanese two-stack Fleet Destroyers. Small one-stackers have many appearance counterparts in all navies among destroyers, torpedo boats, gunboats, and mining craft.

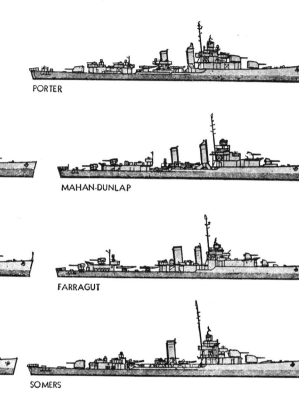

PORTER

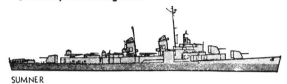

SUMNER

LIVERMORE

FLETCHER

BENSON

MAHAN-DUNLAP

FARRAGUT

SIMS

BENHAM

SOMERS

BAGLEY

100

GRIDLEY

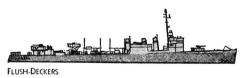

FLUSH-DECKERS

SAMPSON Class
DD 66 ALLEN

No. 75 to 185 Class
DD 106 CHEW
DD 109 CRANE
DD 113 RATHBURNE
DD 118 LEA
DD 126 BADGER
DD 128 BABBITT
DD 138 KENNISON
DD 142 TARBELL
DD 144 UPSHUR
DD 145 GREER
DD 148 BRECKINRIDGE
DD 149 BARNEY
DD 150 BLAKELEY
DD 151 BIDDLE
DD 152 DU PONT
DD 153 BERNADOU
DD 154 ELLIS
DD 155 COLE
DD 156 J. FRED TALBOTT
DD 158 LEARY
DD 159 SCHENCK

No. 186 to 347 Class
DD 186 CLEMSON
DD 187 DAHLGREN
DD 188 GOLDSBOROUGH
DD 196 G. E. BADGER
DD 199 DALLAS
DD 210 BROOME
DD 211 ALDEN

DD 213 BARKER
DD 216 JOHN D. EDWARDS
DD 217 WHIPPLE
DD 218 PARROTT
DD 220 MACLEISH
DD 221 SIMPSON
DD 222 BULMER
DD 223 McCORMICK
DD 228 JOHN D. FORD
DD 230 PAUL JONES
DD 231 HATFIELD
DD 234 FOX
DD 237 McFARLAND
DD 242 KING
DD 244 WILLIAMSON
DD 246 BAINBRIDGE
DD 247 GOFF
DD 248 BARRY
DD 250 LAWRENCE
DD 251 BELKNAP
DD 255 OSMOND INGRAM
DD 266 GREENE
DD 336 LITCHFIELD
DD 341 DECATUR
DD 342 HULBERT

FARRAGUT Class
DD 348 FARRAGUT
DD 349 DEWEY
DD 350 HULL
DD 351 MACDONOUGH
DD 352 WORDEN
DD 353 DALE

DD 354 MONAGHAN
DD 355 AYLWIN

PORTER Class
DD 357 SELFRIDGE
DD 358 McDOUGAL
DD 359 WINSLOW
DD 360 PHELPS
DD 361 CLARK
DD 362 MOFFETT
DD 363 BALCH

MAHAN Class
DD 364 MAHAN
DD 365 CUMMINGS
DD 366 DRAYTON
DD 367 LAMSON
DD 368 FLUSSER
DD 369 REID
DD 370 CASE
DD 371 CONYNGHAM
DD 372 CASSIN
DD 373 SHAW
DD 374 TUCKER
DD 375 DOWNES
DD 377 PERKINS
DD 378 SMITH

DUNLAP Class
DD 384 DUNLAP
DD 385 FANNING

SOMERS Class
DD 381 SOMERS
DD 383 WARRINGTON
DD 394 SAMPSON

DD 395 DAVIS
DD 396 JOUETT

GRIDLEY Class
DD 380 GRIDLEY
DD 382 CRAVEN
DD 400 McCALL
DD 401 MAURY

BAGLEY Class
DD 386 BAGLEY
DD 388 HELM
DD 389 MUGFORD
DD 390 RALPH TALBOT
DD 392 PATTERSON

BENHAM Class
DD 398 ELLET
DD 399 LANG
DD 402 MAYRANT
DD 403 TRIPPE
DD 404 RHIND
DD 406 STACK
DD 407 STERETT
DD 408 WILSON

SIMS Class
DD 410 HUGHES
DD 411 ANDERSON
DD 413 MUSTIN
DD 414 RUSSELL
DD 417 MORRIS
DD 418 ROE
DD 419 WAINWRIGHT

BENSON Class [Numerical Summary: DD 421–428; 459–460; 491–492; 598–617]

DD 421	BENSON
DD 422	MAYO
DD 423	GLEAVES
DD 424	NIBLACK
DD 425	MADISON
DD 426	LANDSDALE
DD 427	HILARY P. JONES
DD 428	CHAS. F. HUGHES
DD 460	WOODWORTH
DD 491	FARENHOLT
DD 492	BAILEY
DD 598	BANCROFT
DD 600	BOYLE
DD 601	CHAMPLIN
DD 602	MEADE
DD 603	MURPHY
DD 604	PARKER
DD 605	CALDWELL
DD 606	COGHLAN
DD 607	FRAZIER
DD 608	GANSEVOORT
DD 609	GILLESPIE
DD 610	HOBBY
DD 611	KALK
DD 612	KENDRICK
DD 613	LAUB
DD 614	MACKENZIE
DD 615	McLANAHAN
DD 616	NIELDS
DD 617	ORDRONAUX

LIVERMORE Class [Numerical Summary: DD 429–444; 453–458; 461–464; 483–490; 493–497; 618–628; 632–641; 645–648]

DD 429	LIVERMORE
DD 430	EBERLE
DD 431	PLUNKETT
DD 432	KEARNY
DD 435	GRAYSON
DD 437	WOOLSEY
DD 438	LUDLOW
DD 439	EDISON
DD 440	ERICSSON
DD 441	WILKES
DD 442	NICHOLSON
DD 443	SWANSON
DD 454	ELLYSON
DD 455	HAMBLETON
DD 456	RODMAN
DD 457	EMMONS
DD 458	MACOMB
DD 461	FORREST
DD 462	FITCH
DD 463	CORRY
DD 464	HOBSON
DD 484	BUCHANAN
DD 486	LANSDOWNE
DD 487	LARDNER
DD 488	McCALLA
DD 489	MERVINE
DD 490	QUICK
DD 493	CARMICK
DD 494	DOYLE
DD 495	ENDICOTT
DD 496	McCOOK
DD 497	FRANKFORD
DD 618	DAVISON
DD 619	EDWARDS
DD 620	GLENNON
DD 621	JEFFERS
DD 623	NELSON
DD 624	BALDWIN
DD 625	HARDING
DD 626	SATTERLEE
DD 627	THOMPSON
DD 628	WELLES
DD 632	COWIE
DD 633	KNIGHT
DD 634	DORAN
DD 635	EARLE
DD 636	BUTLER
DD 637	GHERARDI
DD 638	HERNDON
DD 639	SHUBRICK
DD 641	TILLMAN
DD 645	STEVENSON
DD 646	STOCKTON
DD 647	THORN
DD 648	TURNER

FLETCHER Class [Numerical Summary: DD 445–452; 465–482; 498–502; 507–522; 526–541; 544–547; 550–597; 629–631; 642–644; 649–691]

DD 445	FLETCHER
DD 446	RADFORD
DD 447	JENKINS
DD 448	LAVALLETTE
DD 449	NICHOLAS
DD 450	O'BANNON
DD 452	PERCIVAL
DD 465	SAUFLEY
DD 466	WALLER
DD 468	TAYLOR
DD 470	BACHE
DD 471	BEALE
DD 472	GUEST
DD 473	BENNETT
DD 474	FULLAM
DD 475	HUDSON
DD 476	HUTCHINS
DD 477	PRINGLE
DD 478	STANLY
DD 479	STEVENS
DD 480	HALFORD
DD 481	LEUTZE
DD 482	WATSON
DD 498	PHILIP
DD 499	RENSHAW
DD 500	RINGGOLD
DD 501	SCHROEDER
DD 502	SIGSBEE
DD 507	CONWAY
DD 508	CONY
DD 509	CONVERSE
DD 510	EATON
DD 511	FOOTE
DD 512	SPENCE

FLETCHER Class—Continued.

DD 513	TERRY	
DD 514	THATCHER	
DD 515	ANTHONY	
DD 516	WADSWORTH	
DD 517	WALKER	
DD 518	BROWNSON	
DD 519	DALY	
DD 520	ISHERWOOD	
DD 521	KIMBERLY	
DD 522	LUCE	
DD 526	ABNER READ	
DD 527	AMMEN	
DD 528	MULLANY	
DD 529	BUSH	
DD 530	TRATHEN	
DD 531	HAZELWOOD	
DD 532	HEERMANN	
DD 533	HOEL	
DD 534	McCORD	
DD 535	MILLER	
DD 536	OWEN	
DD 537	THE SULLIVANS	
DD 538	STEPHEN POTTER	
DD 539	TINGEY	
DD 540	TWINING	
DD 541	YARNALL	
DD 544	BOYD	
DD 545	BRADFORD	
DD 546	BROWN	
DD 547	COWELL	
DD 550	CAPPS	

DD 551	DAVID W. TAYLOR	
DD 552	EVANS	
DD 553	JOHN D. HENLEY	
DD 554	FRANKS	
DD 555	HAGGARD	
DD 556	HAILEY	
DD 557	JOHNSTON	
DD 558	LAWS	
DD 559	LONGSHAW	
DD 560	MORRISON	
DD 561	PRICHETT	
DD 562	ROBINSON	
DD 563	ROSS	
DD 564	ROWE	
DD 565	SMALLEY	
DD 566	STODDARD	
DD 567	WATTS	
DD 568	WREN	
DD 569	AULICK	
DD 570	CHAS. AUSBURNE	
DD 571	CLAXTON	
DD 572	DYSON	
DD 573	HARRISON	
DD 574	JOHN RODGERS	
DD 575	McKEE	
DD 576	MURRAY	
DD 577	SPROSTON	
DD 578	WICKES	
DD 579	WM. D. PORTER	
DD 580	YOUNG	
DD 581	CHARRETTE	
DD 582	CONNER	

DD 583	HALL	
DD 584	HALLIGAN	
DD 585	HARADEN	
DD 586	NEWCOMB	
DD 587	BELL	
DD 588	BURNS	
DD 589	IZARD	
DD 590	PAUL HAMILTON	
DD 591	TWIGGS	
DD 592	HOWORTH	
DD 593	KILLEN	
DD 594		
DD 595	METCALFE	
DD 596	SHIELDS	
DD 597	WILEY	
DD 629	ABBOT	
DD 630	BRAINE	
DD 631	ERBEN	
DD 642	HALE	
DD 643	SIGOURNEY	
DD 644	STEMBEL	
DD 649	ALBERT W. GRANT	
DD 650	CAPERTON	
DD 651	COGSWELL	
DD 652	INGERSOLL	
DD 653	KNAPP	
DD 654	BEARSS	
DD 655	JOHN HOOD	
DD 656	VAN VALKEN-BURGH	
DD 657	CHAS. J. BADGER	
DD 658	COLAHAN	

DD 659	DASHIELL	
DD 660	BULLARD	
DD 661	KIDD	
DD 662	BENNION	
DD 663	HEYWOOD L. EDWARDS	
DD 664	RICHARD P. LEARY	
DD 665	BRYANT	
DD 666	BLACK	
DD 667	CHAUNCEY	
DD 668	CLARENCE K. BRONSON	
DD 669	COTTEN	
DD 670	DORTCH	
DD 671	GATLING	
DD 672	HEALY	
DD 673	HICKOX	
DD 674	HUNT	
DD 675	LEWIS HANCOCK	
DD 676	MARSHALL	
DD 677	McDERMUT	
DD 678	McGOWAN	
DD 679	McNAIR	
DD 680	MELVIN	
DD 681	HOPEWELL	
DD 682	PORTERFIELD	
DD 683	STOCKHAM	
DD 684	WEDDERBURN	
DD 685	PICKING	
DD 686	HALSEY POWELL	
DD 687	UHLMANN	
DD 688	REMEY	

FLETCHER Class—Continued.

DD 689 WADLEIGH	DD 704 BORIE	DD 734	DD 764
DD 690 NORMAN SCOTT	DD 705	DD 735	DD 765
DD 691 MERTZ	DD 706	DD 736	DD 766
DD 792 CALLAGHAN	DD 707	DD 737	DD 767
DD 793 CASSIN YOUNG	DD 708	DD 738	DD 768
DD 794 IRWIN	DD 709	DD 739	DD 769
DD 795 PRESTON	DD 710	DD 740	DD 770 LOWRY
DD 796 BENHAM	DD 711	DD 741	DD 771 LINDSEY
DD 797 CUSHING	DD 712	DD 742	DD 772 GWIN
DD 798 MONSSEN	DD 713	DD 743	DD 773 AARON WARD
DD 799 JARVIS	DD 714	DD 744 BLUE	DD 774
DD 800 PORTER	DD 715	DD 745 BRUSH	DD 775
DD 801 COLHOUN	DD 716	DD 746 TAUSSIG	DD 776
DD 802 GREGORY	DD 717	DD 747 SAMUEL N. MOORE	DD 777
DD 803 LITTLE	DD 718	DD 748 HARRY E. HUBBARD	DD 778
DD 804 ROOKS	DD 719	DD 749 HENRY A. WILEY	DD 779

Sumner Class

	DD 720	DD 750	DD 780
DD 692 ALLEN M. SUMNER	DD 721	DD 751	DD 781
DD 693 MOALE	DD 722 BARTON	DD 752	DD 782
DD 694 INGRAHAM	DD 723 WALKE	DD 753	DD 783
DD 695 COOPER	DD 724 LAFFEY	DD 754	DD 784
DD 696 ENGLISH	DD 725 O'BRIEN	DD 755	DD 785
DD 697 CHARLES S. SPERRY	DD 726 MEREDITH	DD 756	DD 786
DD 698 AULT	DD 727 DEHAVEN	DD 757 PUTNAM	DD 787
DD 699 WALDRON	DD 728 MANSFIELD	DD 758 STRONG	DD 788
DD 700	DD 729 LYMAN K. SWENSON	DD 759	DD 789
DD 701	DD 730 COLLETT	DD 760	DD 790
DD 702	DD 731 MADDOX	DD 761	DD 791
DD 703	DD 732 HYMAN	DD 762	DD 805 to 890 incl.
	DD 733 MANNERT L. ABELE	DD 763	

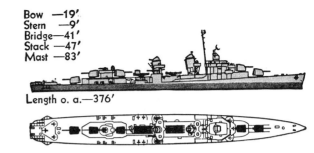

Bow —19'
Stern —9'
Bridge—41'
Stack —47'
Mast —83'

Length o. a.—376'

Observer's Note:
—Flush, broad-beamed hull.
—Two broad, raking stacks; 2-A-1-2 gunhouse disposition.
—May be mistaken for German NARVIKS, Japanese Fleet Destroyers, or U. S. Light Cruisers.

Photos are of MILLER, TRATHEN, and DASHIELL.

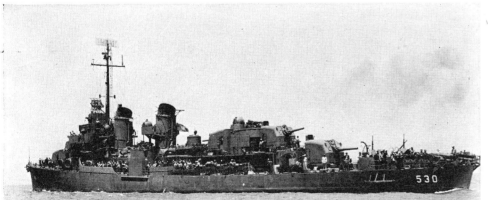

FLETCHER Class—DD

▲ MILLER, 9–21–43   ▼ CHAUNCERY, 8–14–43.   On opposite page McCORD, MILLER, and COLTEN.

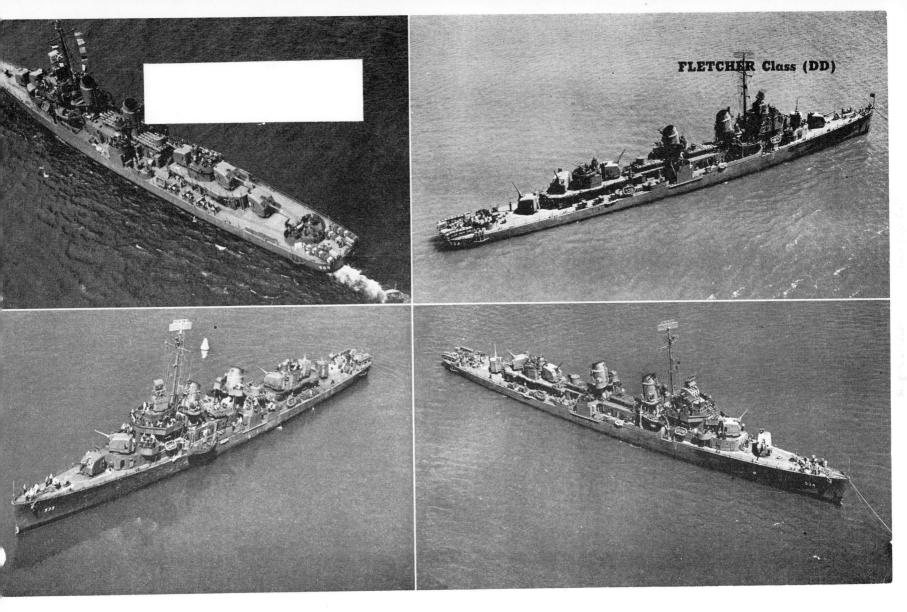

FLETCHER Class (DD)

The twin 5"/38 mounts illustrated also form the standard secondary battery seen on all our new BB's, CA's, and CL's.   All photos are of the BARTON, taken 12-29-43.

Bow	—20'
Stern	—10'
Bridge	—35'
Stack	—46'
Mast	—84'

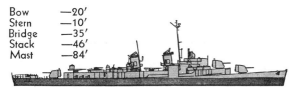

Length o. a.—376'

Observer's Note:
—Similar to FLETCHER's in profile.   Note continuous deck-house.
—2–A–1 (twin) shield arrangement.
—Arrangement of torpedo battery and AAMG positions is distinctive from the air.

BENSON, LIVERMORE Classes—DD

Surface views are of the GLENNON, one of the LIVERMORE group. A typical BENSON unit is illustrated by the aerial photographs. All photos 1943.

Surface views are of the GLENNON, one of the LIVERMORE group. A typical BENSON unit is illustrated by the aerial photographs. All photos 1943.

BENSON, LIVERMORE Classes—DD

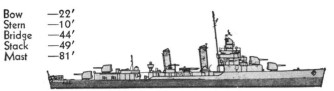

Bow —22'
Stern —10'
Bridge —44'
Stack —49'
Mast —81'

Length o. a.—348'

These ships were designed with two quintuple torpedo mounts (still retained on some ships) and five 5-inch shielded mounts—since reduced for AA positions.

Observer's Note:
—Two thin raking stacks—round in LIVERMORE's, square in BENSON's.
—Closely resemble all Japanese two-stack fleet destroyers.

◄ BAILEY, photo 9-3-42, of the BENSON Class. ▼ SWANSON, a LIVERMORE unit, carrying full torpedo armament.

SIMS Class—DD

As in other destroyer classes, recent AA armament changes create minor differences between sister ships. Note that No. 3 gun position is an open or side-shielded mount. Photos—ROE, 9-13-43, and ANDERSON, 5-21-43.

SIMS Class—DD

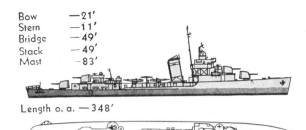

Bow	—21'
Stern	—11'
Bridge	—49'
Stack	—49'
Mast	—83'

Length o. a. —348'

Observer's Note:
—Single, large, raking stack (capped).
—Distinguished from other one-stackers by center-line torpedo battery and bridge-foremast arrangement.

▼ Photo shows SIMS, BENHAM, and LIVERMORE units. Notice the great similarity between the one-stackers. These two classes are often consolidated for recognition purposes.

▲ STACK, 8-6-42. Notice that on some units the original open gun mounts are still carried aft. ▼ RHIND, 9-17-42.

Bow —22'
Stern —10'
Bridge —43'
Stack —48'
Mast —86'

Length o. a.—341'

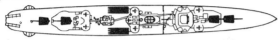

Observer's Note:
—Large single trunked stack (no stack cap).
—Amidships quadruple torpedo mount differentiate these ships from SIMS, GRIDLEY, BAGLEY Classes.

◀ RHIND, 9-17-42.   USS TRIPPE, 6-3-42. ▼

◄ GRIDLEY,
11–12–42

Also opposite
page.

◄ McCALL,
11–12–42

◄ CRAVEN,
5–10–42

Bow	—22'
Stern	—10'
Bridge	—43'
Stack	—46'
Mast	—95'

Length o. a. —341'

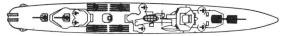

Observer's Note:

—Excessive trunking of stack distinguishes ships of this class from the other One-stackers.

—The British J–T Classes, newer Italian designs, and the Japanese TERUTSUKI's resemble this class.

Bow   —20'
Stern —10'
Bridge —45'
Stack —50'
Mast   —84'

Length o. a. —341'

Observers's Note:
—Widely split trunked stack and paired quadruple torpedo tubes differentiate these ships from the BENHAM–SIMS Classes.
—2–A–2 gun arrangement—shields forward, open mount aft.
—Note great similarity to the GRIDLEY Class in all details.

▼ RALPH TALBOT, 12-42.

▲ WARRINGTON 4–23–43 and SAMPSON ▼ 3–14–43 show recent main battery changes, typical of some units.

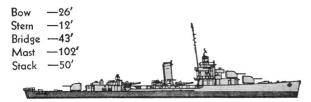

Bow —26'
Stern —12'
Bridge —43'
Mast —102'
Stack —50'

Length o. a.—381'

Observer's Note:
—Distinctive tall, raking, single-pipe stack.
—Similar in other details to the Porter Class.
—Recent AAMG additions have reduced main battery (twins) arrangement from 2–A–2, as illustrated below, to 2–A–1 shown on opposite page.

DD 395—DAVIS

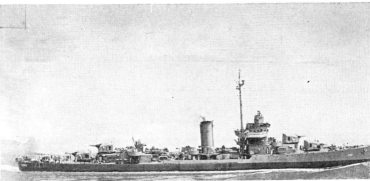

DUNLAP ▲ and FLUSSER ▼ illustrates appearance differences in the two combined classes.

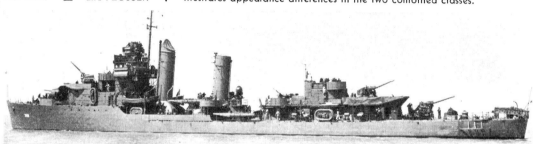

◄ The rebuilt CASSIN and DOWNES constitute a new variation in this class. CUSHING ▼

MAHAN-DUNLAP Classes—DD

Bow	—22'
Stern	—10'
Bridge	—43'
Stack	—55'
Mast	—84'

Length o. a.—341'

Observer's Note:

—Gunhouses forward differentiate DUNLAP from MAHAN Class (open gunshields).

—Very similar in appearance to PORTER, LIVERMORE, BENSON Classes; differentiated by armament disposition and stack spacing.

—May be mistaken for all new Japanese 2-stack DDS.

◀ CONYNGHAM, 1-42   ▼ FLUSSER, 1-43

▼ PHELPS, 12-11-42.　　　▼ McDOUGAL, 8-12-42.　　　MOFFETT, 10-28-42. ▶

PORTER Class—DD

Bow	—24'
Stern	—12'
Bridge	—46'
Stack	—55'
Mast	—81'

Length o. a.—381'

Observer's Note:

—Two raking single-pipe stacks (cowl on No. 1 stack).

—Recently authorized AAMG additions will change all main battery dispositions to 2-A-1 (twins).

—Very similar to MAHAN in appearance since recent alterations.

▲ PHELPS, 5-26-43.　　▼ McDOUGAL, 8-12-42.

AYLWYN, 1-43.   Recent alterations in armament are circled on detail view.

FARRAGUT Class—DD

Bow	—21'
Stern	—10'
Bridge	—43'
Stack	—48'
Mast	—85'

Length o. a.—341'

Observer's Note:
—Two closely spaced stacks of unequal thickness.
—Shielded superimposed mounts forward, open guns aft.
—Two in-line torpedo mounts on main deck abaft stack.
—Resembles all Japanese 2-stack destroyers and mine-sweepers, also many British types.

◀ DEWEY, 12-42   ▼ WORDEN, 1-43.

FLUSH DECKERS—DD

All units have had their stacks lowered; only a few, like BAINBRIDGE retain the original four.   The shielding of the 3-inch guns and AA armament differ among ships of this class.

FLUSH DECKERS—DD

The building program of 1917–21 produced a large fleet of "flush deck" destroyers. Many of these have been scrapped or wrecked. Others, after modification and conversion, have been given special assignments with the fleet.

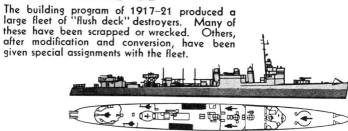

Those retained as Destroyers by the Navy have almost all been altered to three stacks with a modified armament arrangement amidship.

In September 1940, 50 went to the United Kingdom in exchange for naval bases, and were renamed for cities common to both Great Britain and the United States. While alterations were made by the British, including reduction of stacks to three in some ships, these retain their original appearance more than any others. ▼

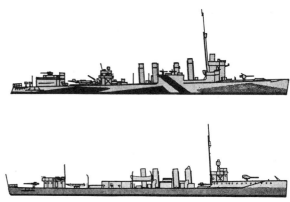

ALLEN—DD 66

The ALLEN is the only remaining vessel of the high-forecastled "1,000-tonners" built in 1917. It is still on Fleet duty; displaces 920 tons, is 315 feet, 3 inches overall.

APD—High-Speed (Destroyer) Transports

The forward boilers and stacks have been removed for accommodation space; heavy davits and AA positions added. Twenty-three units were converted, beginning in 1938; others are planned.

AVD—Seaplane Tender (Destroyer)

The forward two stacks and boilers have been removed, bridge structure extended aft across well and armament and deck aft greatly altered. As these ships are replaced by the new AVP's, they will be transferred to DD or APD duty.

DM—Light Minelayer

Number 4 stack removed and torpedo armament replaced with antiaircraft positions and minelaying gear. Eight units converted, 1930–37—more are planned.

DMS—High-Speed Minesweepers

Converted similar to the DM, except that sweeping gear is installed aft. Seventeen vessels were converted, beginning in 1940, others are now undergoing conversion.

U. S. SUBMARINES

U. S. SUBMARINES

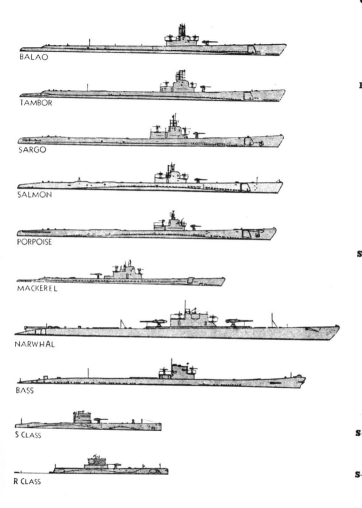

BALAO

TAMBOR

SARGO

SALMON

PORPOISE

MACKEREL

NARWHAL

BASS

S CLASS

R CLASS

LIST BY CLASSES

O-1 Class
SS 63   O-2
SS 64   O-3
SS 65   O-4
SS 67   O-6
SS 68   O-7
SS 69   O-8
SS 71   O-10

R-1 Class
SS 78   R-1
SS 79   R-2
SS 81   R-4
SS 82   R-5
SS 83   R-6
SS 84   R-7
SS 86   R-9
SS 87   R-10
SS 88   R-11
SS 90   R-13
SS 91   R-14
SS 92   R-15
SS 93   R-16
SS 95   R-18
SS 97   R-20

S-1 Class
SS 123   S-18
SS 125   S-20
SS 128   S-23
SS 132   S-27
SS 133   S-28
SS 135   S-30
SS 136   S-31
SS 137   S-32
SS 138   S-33
SS 139   S-34
SS 140   S-35
SS 142   S-37
SS 143   S-38
SS 144   S-39
SS 145   S-40
SS 146   S-41

S-3 Class
SS 116   S-11
SS 117   S-12
SS 118   S-13

S-14 Class
SS 119   S-14

S-14 Class—Continued
SS 120   S-15
SS 121   S-16
SS 122   S-17

S-42 Class
SS 153   S-42
SS 154   S-43
SS 156   S-45
SS 157   S-46
SS 158   S-47
SS 159   S-48

BARRACUDA Class
SS 163   BARRACUDA
SS 164   BASS
SS 165   BONITA

NARWHAL Class
SS 167   NARWHAL
SS 168   NAUTILUS
SS 169   DOLPHIN

CACHALOT Class
SS 170   CACHALOT
SS 171   CUTTLEFISH

PORPOISE Class
SS 172   PORPOISE
SS 173   PIKE
SS 175   TARPON
SS 178   PERMIT
SS 179   PLUNGER
SS 180   POLLACK

SALMON Class
SS 182   SALMON
SS 183   SEAL
SS 184   SKIPJACK
SS 185   SNAPPER
SS 186   STINGRAY
SS 187   STURGEON

SARGO Class
SS 188   SARGO
SS 189   SAURY
SS 190   SPEARFISH
SS 191   SCUPLIN
SS 192   SAILFISH
SS 193   SWORDFISH
SS 194   SEADRAGON
SS 196   SEARAVEN
SS 197   SEAWOLF

MACKEREL Class
(experimental boats)
SS 204   MACKEREL
SS 205   MARLIN

TAMBOR Class
SS 198   TAMBOR
SS 199   TAUTOG
SS 200   THRESHER
SS 202   TROUT
SS 203   TUNA
SS 206   GAR
SS 208   GRAYBACK
SS 211   GUDGEON
SS 212   GATO
SS 213   GREENLING
SS 214   GROUPER
SS 215   GROWLER
SS 217   GUARDFISH
SS 218   ALBACORE
SS 220   BARB
SS 221   BLACKFISH
SS 222   BLUEFISH
SS 223   BONEFISH
SS 224   COD
SS 225   CERO
SS 226   CORVINA
SS 227   DARTER
SS 228   DRUM
SS 229   FLYING FISH
SS 230   FINBACK
SS 231   HADDOCK
SS 232   HALIBUT
SS 233   HERRING
SS 234   KINGFISH
SS 235   SHAD
SS 236   SILVERSIDES
SS 237   TRIGGER
SS 239   WHALE
SS 240   ANGLER
SS 241   BASHAW
SS 242   BLUEGILL
SS 243   BREAM
SS 244   CAVALLA
SS 245   COBIA
SS 246   CROAKER
SS 247   DACE

TAMBOR Class—Continued

SS 249	FLASHER
SS 250	FLIER
SS 251	FLOUNDER
SS 252	GABILAN
SS 253	GUNNEL
SS 254	GURNARD
SS 255	HADDO
SS 256	HAKE
SS 257	HARDER
SS 258	HOE
SS 259	JACK
SS 260	LAPON
SS 261	MINGO
SS 262	MUSKALLUNGE
SS 263	PADDLE
SS 264	PARGO
SS 265	PETO
SS 266	POGY
SS 267	POMPON
SS 268	PUFFER
SS 269	RASHER
SS 270	RATON
SS 271	RAY
SS 272	REDFIN
SS 273	ROBALO
SS 274	ROCK
SS 276	SAWFISH
SS 277	SCAMP
SS 278	SCORPION
SS 279	SNOOK
SS 280	STEELHEAD
SS 281	SUNFISH
SS 282	TUNNY
SS 283	TINOSA
SS 284	TULLIBEE

BALAO Class

SS 285	BALAO
SS 286	BILLFISH
SS 287	BOWFIN
SS 288	CABRILLA
SS 289	CAPELIN
SS 291	CREVALLE
SS 292	DEVILFISH
SS 293	DRAGONET
SS 294	ESCOLAR

BALAO Class—Continued

SS 295	HACKLEBACK
SS 296	LANCETFISH
SS 297	LING
SS 298	LIONFISH
SS 299	MANTA
SS 300	MORAY
SS 301	RONCADOR
SS 302	SABALO
SS 303	SABLEFISH
SS 304	SEAHORSE
SS 305	SKATE
SS 306	TANG
SS 307	TILEFISH
SS 308	APOGON
SS 309	ASPRO
SS 310	BATFISH
SS 311	ARCHER FISH
SS 312	BURRFISH
SS 313	PERCH
SS 314	SHARK
SS 315	SEA LION
SS 316	BARBAL
SS 317	BARBERO
SS 318	BAYA
SS 319	BECUNA
SS 320	BERGALL
SS 321	BESUGO
SS 322	BLACKFIN
SS 323	CAIMAN
SS 324	BLENNY
SS 325	BLOWER
SS 326	BLUEBACK
SS 327	BOARFISH
SS 328	CHARR
SS 329	CHUBB
SS 330	BRILL
SS 331	BUGARA
SS 332	BULLHEAD
SS 333	BUMPER
SS 334	CABEZON
SS 335	DENTUDA
SS 336	CAPITAINE
SS 337	CARBONERO
SS 338	CARP
SS 339	CATFISH
SS 340	ENTEMEDOR
SS 341	CHIVO

BALAO Class—Continued

SS 342	CHOPPER
SS 343	CLAMAGORE
SS 344	COBBLER
SS 345	COCHINO
SS 346	CORPORAL
SS 347	CUBERA
SS 348	CUSK
SS 349	DIODON
SS 350	DOGFISH
SS 351	GREENFISH
SS 352	HALFBEAK
SS 353	DUGONG
SS 354	EEL
SS 355	ESPADA
SS 356	JAWFISH
SS 357	ONO
SS 358	GARLOPA
SS 359	GARRUPA
SS 360	GOLDRING
SS 361	GOLET
SS 362	GUAVINA
SS 363	GUITARRO
SS 364	HAMMERHEAD
SS 365	HARDHEAD
SS 366	HAWKBILL
SS 367	ICEFISH
SS 368	JALLAO
SS 369	KETE
SS 370	KRAKEN
SS 371	LARGARTO
SS 372	LAMPREY
SS 373	LIZARDFISH
SS 374	LOGGERHEAD
SS 375	MACABI
SS 376	MAPIRO
SS 377	MENHADEN
SS 378	MERO
SS 379	NEEDLEFISH
SS 380	NERKA
SS 381	SAND LANCE
SS 382	PICUDA
SS 383	PAMPANITO
SS 384	PARCHE
SS 385	BANG
SS 386	PILOTFISH
SS 387	PINTADO
SS 388	PIPEFISH

BALAO Class—Continued

SS 389	PIRANHA
SS 390	PLAICE
SS 391	POMFRET
SS 392	STERLET
SS 393	QUEENFISH
SS 394	RAZORBACK
SS 395	REDFISH
SS 396	RONQUIL
SS 397	SCABBARDFISH
SS 398	SEGUNDO
SS 399	SEA CAT
SS 400	SEA DEVIL
SS 401	SEA DOG
SS 402	SEA FOX
SS 403	ATULE
SS 404	SPIKEFISH
SS 405	SEA OWL
SS 406	SEA POACHER
SS 407	SEA ROBIN
SS 408	SENNET
SS 409	AWA
SS 410	THREADFIN
SS 411	SPADEFISH
SS 412	TREPANG
SS 413	SPOT
SS 414	SPRINGER
SS 415	STICKLEBACK
SS 416	TIRU
SS 417	TENCH
SS 418	THORNBACK
SS 419	TIGRONE
SS 420	TIRANTE
SS 421	TRUTTA
SS 422	TORO
SS 423	TORSK
SS 424	TREMBLER
SS 425	TRUMPETFISH
SS 426	TUSK
SS 427	TURBOT
SS 428	ULNA
SS 429	UNICORN
SS 430	VENDACE
SS 431	WALRUS
SS 432	WHITEFISH
SS 433	WHITING
SS 434	WOLFFISH
SS 435–544	

BALAO Class   The BALAO represents the newest type of U. S. fleet submarine, distinguished by an extremely low conning tower, and tall heavy periscope shears. (Also a characteristic of Italian submarines.)   ▼ SS 305—SKATE—8-28-43.

▼ Views showing different stages of submerging.　　　▲ SS 288 CABRILLA—photos taken at 150-foot altitude.

FLEET SUBMARINES—TAMBOR • SARGO • SALMON • PORPOISE Classes

Fleet submarines follow a standard design, with improvements and modifications occurring in successive classes, which may be identified only by closely observing minor details, such as fantail and after deck variations. All are 300 to 312 feet overall.

▼ SS 178 PERMIT, of the PORPOISE Class. Note new deck bow tubes.

▲ SS 199 TAUTOG and SS 208 GRAYBACK, ▲ both TAMBOR Class units.

TAMBOR · SARGO · SALMON · PORPOISE Classes

SS 208 GRAYBACK, of the TAMBOR Class. ▼

▼ SS 184 SKIPJACK, of the SALMON Class.

▲ SS 193 SWORDFISH, of the SARGO Class.

FLEET SUBMARINES

Seen from the air, new U. S. submarines resemble one another closely. The fore and aft conning tower step is, however, a distinctive feature of U. S. design. Except for this they may easily be mistaken for the Japanese "I" types. All photos here are of subs of the new TAMBOR Class.

▲ SS 242 BLUEGILL. Photographed 11-24-43 at 400-foot altitude.
▼ SS 254 GURNARD. This photo shows the original conning tower design and the after deck gun location—still retained by some units.

▼ SS 277 SCAMP. Note the prominent pressure-hull and characteristic stern.

NARWHAL Class

These ships are among the largest submarines in the world, displacing 2,730 tons surfaced, 3,960 tons submerged, with 371 feet length overall. Modernization includes additional stern deck tubes and a lower conning tower. Original deck armament is retained. NAUTILUS has deck tubes immediately abaft conning tower, NARWHAL'S tubes are located on the fantail.

▲ NAUTILUS—Photo 9-3-43—Note deck bow tubes.　　　▼ NARWHAL—Photo 4-3-43, showing prominent stern deck tubes.

Experimental submarines now employed as schoolships.

▼ SS 169—DOLPHIN, completed in 1932. Length 319 feet, displacement 1,540 tons.

▲ SS 204—MACKEREL and SS 205—MARLIN ▲ 243-foot, 800-ton long-range submarines. The MACKEREL has retained its original conning tower.

Completed between 1916–1918, this class is usually split into "Government" and "Holland" types. Of the latter group, three appearance types are illustrated on these pages.

Photos, all taken in 1943, show new alterations in the conning tower, machine gun location and the stern deck structure.

BASS, O Classes—SS   BASS Class, SS 163–165, completed in 1926, were the first large modern U. S. submarines.

▲ "O" Class submarines, SS 63–71, World War I craft, now used only for training   Length 172 feet.

▲▼ Photos show reconditioned BASS Class unit.

"R" Class submarines, World War I designs, are now used as training ships or have been lend-leased to the British.
▲ SS 78, R-1, shown without deck armament, differs from the other ships in this class, whose appearance is illustrated by R-2. ▼

TYPICAL CONNING TOWER

Before the outbreak of the present war, U. S. submarines were easily recognized by certain specific characteristics. Conning towers were distinctive, deck guns were always aft..

Late in 1942, however, conning tower height was reduced with a fore and aft step as shown, creating a smaller silhouette and more AA clearance, and the deck gun was moved forward of the conning tower. These characteristics are now standard for all U. S. fleet submarines. The general design, however, has recently been paralleled by some German U-boat types. ▶

U. S. MINOR COMBATANT TYPES

PATROL CRAFT

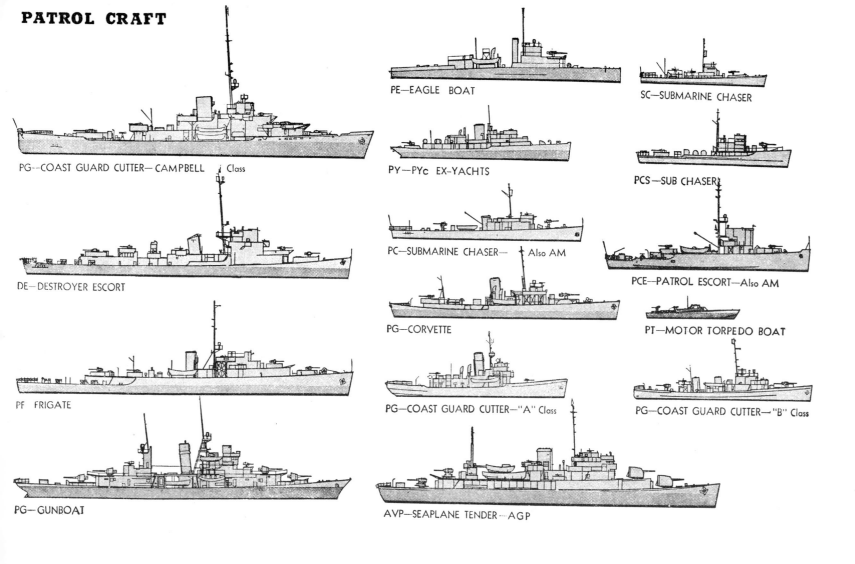

PG—COAST GUARD CUTTER—CAMPBELL Class

DE—DESTROYER ESCORT

PF FRIGATE

PG—GUNBOAT

PE—EAGLE BOAT

PY—PYc EX-YACHTS

PC—SUBMARINE CHASER— Also AM

PG—CORVETTE

PG—COAST GUARD CUTTER—"A" Class

AVP—SEAPLANE TENDER—AGP

SC—SUBMARINE CHASER

PCS—SUB CHASER

PCE—PATROL ESCORT—Also AM

PT—MOTOR TORPEDO BOAT

PG—COAST GUARD CUTTER—"B" Class

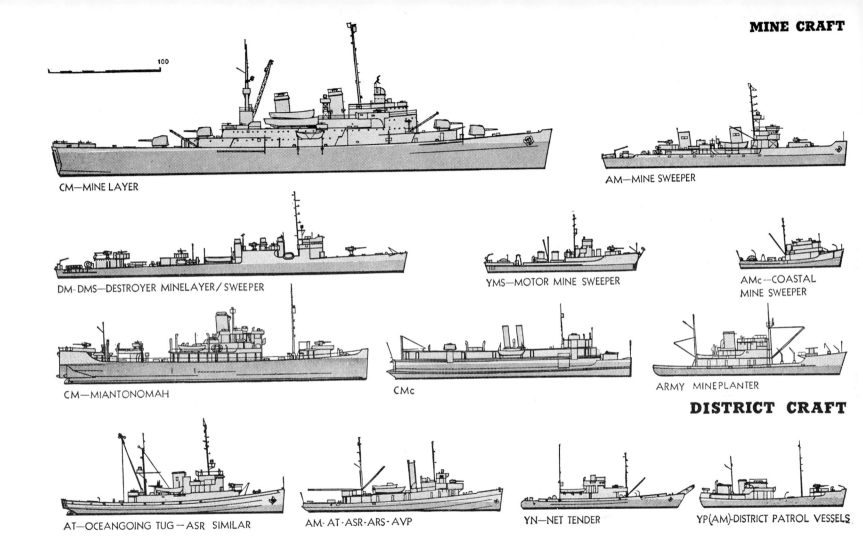

100

CM—MINE LAYER

AM—MINE SWEEPER

DM-DMS—DESTROYER MINELAYER/SWEEPER

YMS—MOTOR MINE SWEEPER

AMc—COASTAL MINE SWEEPER

CM—MIANTONOMAH

CMc

ARMY MINEPLANTER

DISTRICT CRAFT

AT—OCEANGOING TUG - ASR SIMILAR

AM- AT -ASR-ARS- AVP

YN—NET TENDER

YP(AM)—DISTRICT PATROL VESSELS

McCONNELL, 6-43

▲ BUCKLEY, 5-33

Bow	—20'
Stern	—9'
Bridge	—40'
Stack	—40'
Mast	—85'

Length o. a.—306'

These ships still retain many of the attributes of the destroyers they replace in escort duties. Torpedo armament differentiates them from the short-hull DE's.

Observer's Note:
—Long-hull DE's have either a raking single pipe or trunked stack, depending upon type of drive. Although no class differentiation is made, these ships are classified under four separate groups, according to builder and machinery.

◀ REUBEN JAMES, 4-43   ▼ ACREE, 8-43

EVARTS Class-(DE)

All Photos of DE 50—ENGSTROM and DE 14-DOHERTY.

More units of this type are building for both the British and U. S. Navy.

EVARTS Class—DE

Bow	—18'
Stern	—10'
Bridge	—43'
Stack	—40'
Mast	—90'

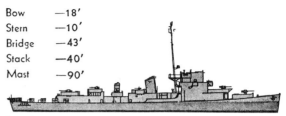

Length o. a.—289'

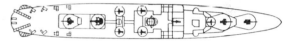

Built for the British as frigates (Captain Class)—some units have been retained by our Navy. As in the long-hull type, power is either steam or diesel.

Observer's Notes:
—Flush hull, continuous deckhouse, short raked stack, pole mast.
—Absence of torpedo armament differentiates this from BUCKLEY Class.

FRIGATES (PF)

▲ PF 37—SAN PEDRO and PF 2—NATCHEZ ▼ illustrate the destroyer-like appearance of this design. Note hull is broken aft, and that stack is not supported by any superstructure.

British RIVER Class sloop, illustrating the type of vessel from which the U. S. Frigates were developed. ▲

▲ Two of these were taken over by the Navy and at first designated PG 101 and 102, now as PF 1 and 2.

FRIGATES—PF

A new U. S. Navy-type, these 301-foot Frigates, have been developed from the British "RIVER Class" sloop. The United States Maritime Commission building program involves slight changes in armament and super structure.

Minor AAMG additions are planned.

▼ TACOMA illustrates the new design.

PF3

PG 64—SPRY, a unit of the TEMPTRESS Class.   Photo 8–20–43. ▼   ▲ HMS CLARKIA and ORCHIS ▲ British FLOWER Class sisterships.

A third type with short fore-castle, called the "Canadian" type, is found only in the Royal Navy (silhouette).

This class of gunboats is composed of Canadian-built corvettes procured by the Navy. They are sister ships of the British FLOWER Class ships, measure 205 feet overall, and displace 1,250 tons. Variations exist between the types in our service, as illustrated by the photos. A new group (PG 86–100), will have minor differences in superstructure and armament.

▼ PG 71—TENACITY. All ships are to be changed to this rig, new Radar installed.

▲ All other photos IMPULSE—PG 68—8-27-42.

▲ SS SURVEYOR and EXPLORER are representative of U. S. Coast and Geodetic Survey vessels in non-military status.

Five similar Naval vessels are designated AGS　　▲ SS EXPLORER

▲ PG 72—NOURMAHAL, formerly U. S. C. G. vessel. Tonnage, 1,969. PG 17—DUBUQUE, ex-AG 6; length overall, 200 feet. PADUCAH ▽ similar in appearance.

▲ PG 51—CHARLESTON. Navy-built; carries seaplane. Length overall, 328 feet.
▽ PG 53—VIXEN, ex-ORION. Length overall, 333 feet.

▲ AGS 2—HYDROGRAPHER, a surveying ship. Length overall, 164 feet.

Included in a group of vessels either used as PG's or greatly resembling this type, are former private yachts, commercial surveying ships, cable ships, and old gunboats, all of which have been pressed into war service.

PG 59—SAN BERNADINO. ▶
1,500 tons displacement.

IX 71—KAILUA. Used as a cable ship. Length overall, 174 feet.
▼ Photo 7-17-43.

▲ PG 60—BEAUMONT, ex-yacht CAROLA. Length overall, 226 feet.
▼ AGP 3—JAMESTOWN, ex-PG 58. Length overall, 294 feet.

PG 22—TULSA. Length overall, 241 feet. SACRAMENTO is similar.
▼ Photo 6-24-43.

▲ PY 18—TOURMALINE. Length overall, 182 feet.

▲ PY 21—RUBY, photographed 3-8-43. PY 19—CARNELIAN is similar.
Length overall, 190 feet.

▲ PY 25—CRYSTAL. PY 14—ARGUS, and PY 22—AZURLITE, are similar.
Length overall, 185 feet.
▼ PY 24—ALMANDITE. Length overall, 185 feet.

▲ PG 54—ST. AUGUSTINE, ex-yacht NOPARO. 1,300 tons.

▼ PY 29—MIZPAH. Length overall, 181 feet.

PY's include yachts 500–1,000 tons; PYc's yachts under 500 tons. Several PYc's were formerly classified as PC's; and are now used for coastal and harbor patrol. Vessels are shown as a typical, rather than a comprehensive, coverage. Included also are the 8 World War I Eagle Boats, now used entirely for training.

▲ PE 19—57.

▲ PY 10—ISABEL.

▲ PY 16—ZIRCON, 235'oa. ▼ AGS 3—OCEANOGRAPHER, 293'oa.

▼ PYc 50—STURDY, 154'oa. ▲ PYc 51—VALIANT, 150'oa.

▲ PYc 28—ABILITY. Length overall, 133 feet.

▲ YP 552—ex-yacht TAORMINA. Length overall, 113 feet.

▲ PY 27—GIRASOL; PY 18—TURQUOISE is similar. Length, 170 feet.
▼ PYc 46—IMPETUOUS, ex-PC 454. Length overall, 121 feet.

▲ PYc 36—PARAGON. Length overall, 138 feet.
▼ PYc 16—CHALCEDONY. Length overall, 195 feet.

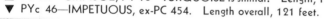

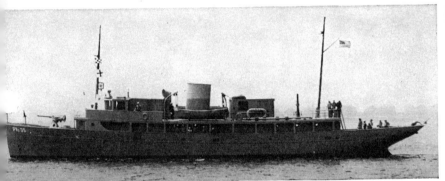

Smaller yachts of many types have been converted to minor combatant vessels in the Navy, Coast Guard, and Army, and are used extensively for coastal patrol or limited escort duty. Shown here are typical yachts of around 500 tons or less, usually assigned for general coastal patrol as PY, PYc, or YP. Many have retained their original names. Many ships of this type are being laid up or returned to their original owner.

▲ PYc 3—AMETHYST.   Length overall, 147 feet.

▲ PYc 35—FELICIA.   Length overall, 147 feet.
▼ PYc 26—CYMOPHANE.   Length overall, 158 feet.

▲ PYc 45—BLACK DOUGLAS.   Length, 153 feet.   Photo 3-30-43.
▼ PYc 44—PERSEVERANCE, ex-Coast Guard vessel BEDFORD.   Photo 3-6-43.

All photos PCE 831. Some units are to be converted to degaussing vessel, logistics support ship, and mine retriever.

ESCORT VESSELS
PCE • PCE(R) • AM

Built for general escort duty, the 180-foot PCE is one of the newest craft to join the Fleet. Note unique superstructure, broken deck line. As PCE(R), this craft is used for rescue work in combat theatres. It has modified full-width superstructure, extending aft to present No. 2 gun position.

ADMIRAL class (AM variation) ▶

▼ BEC 1, typical of lend-lease units.

SUBMARINE CHASERS–PC
173-foot Type

PC 451 and 452 (silhouette) are experimental ships. Others formerly classed as PC's are now reclassified as PY's. The PC 461 class design, after minor alterations, is now used extensively as a minesweeper, known as the ADROIT Class—AM. Both types are in service with the United Nations.

Inset above shows modified PC used as ADROIT Class—AM. ▶

▲ PC 451 Class, an experimental type.

This design along with the SC and Sub-busters, has often been mistaken for submarines, because of their low silhouette and peculiar wake at high speed.

SUBMARINE CHASERS—
110-foot Type

Some of this type are in other United Nations service. Also listed are several Canadian-built FAIRMILES (silhouette), known as SC 1466 Class, and a few experimental types of which SC 450 (silhouette) is typical. Some World War I Units of similar design are still in operation.

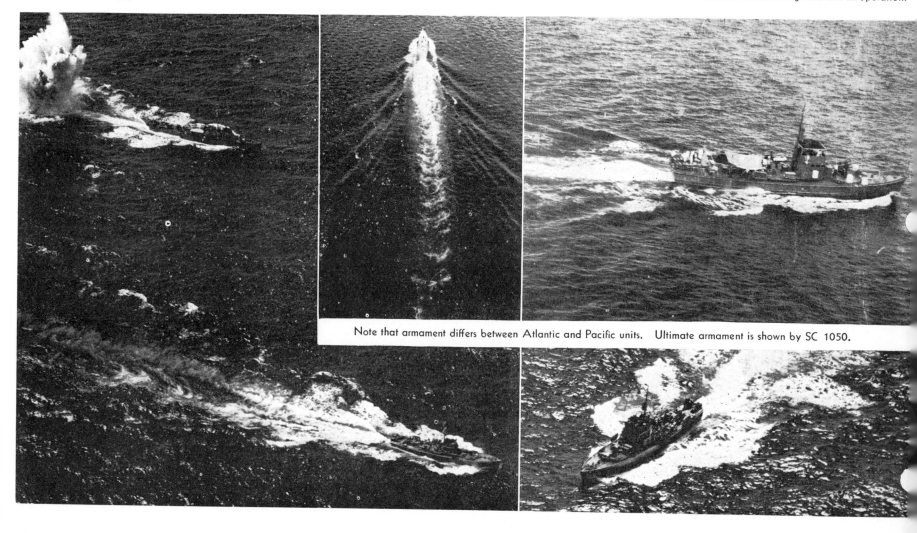

Note that armament differs between Atlantic and Pacific units. Ultimate armament is shown by SC 1050.

SC 450  FAIRMILE

PGM–Motor Gunboats New variation of the SC design used as support craft for landing operations, and offensively, as anti-landing craft gunboats.

▲ PT 103 Class, shown during high-speed trials. Note variance in armament
▼ and torpedo layout—also new radar.

▲ Some boats have been equipped with a 40 mm. single mount on the stern
for anti-landing craft operation.

▼ PT 103 Class, showing typical torpedo boat hull shape.

⬍ 80-foot PT 103 Class.

MOTOR TORPEDO BOATS—PT

Two classes are now in production—the PT 103 Class; 80-foot Elco-built craft, and the PT 71 Class; 78-foot Higgins-built boats. They operate from AGP (Oyster Bay Class ships, converted LST's, or ex-PG's) or land bases. Also in service with other United Nations forces.

▲ PT 103 Class boat—equipped with depth charges.

▲ PT 71 Class boat.

PT wakes have often been confused with that of submarines except at full speed. ▼

▲ PT 20 Class (discontinued). ▼ PT 95 Class—Hutchins built.

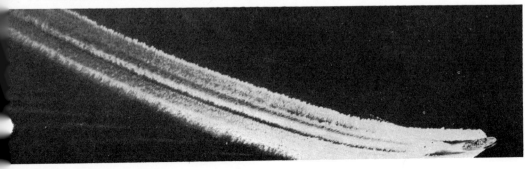

MINELAYERS • CM • CMc

CM 5—TERROR, Navy-built 6,000-ton minelayer. Overall length, 453 feet, 10 inches. Photos 8-24-42.

Two sisterships designed as netlayers have been converted to transports (AP 106 —OZARK, AP 107—CATSKILL). Other ships similar in appearance are the APA I, II—DOYEN Class.

CMc 3 (Coastal Minelayer) WASSUC, displacement, 1,829 tons is shown on the Index Chart.

Five other CM's have been converted from merchant vessels. Largely used for coastal defensive work, they are also available for limited deep-sea operations. Three were formerly train ferries, two were cargo vessels.

MIANTONOMAH—Length overall 292 feet; displacement, 3,638 tons. Sister ship MONADNOCK differs slightly in aft armament. ▶

▼ CM 12—WEEHAWKEN. Length overall, 350 feet; displacement, 5,300 tons.

▲ CM 8—KEOKUK, now AKN—4, and sister ship SALEM, CM—11, differ slightly in mast arrangement. ▼

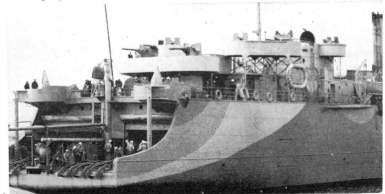

DM • DMS • APD • AVD

Converted from the 1919 flush-deck destroyers are the DM—Light Minelayers, DMS—Fast Minesweeper, APD—High-speed assault Transports and the AVD—Seaplane Tenders. Both DM and DMS have had after stack removed, torpedo armament replaced by mining or sweeping gear. The APD and AVD have had the two forward boilers and stacks removed, landing craft davits or additional accommodations added.

CONVERTED DESTROYERS

APD—MANLEY Class

DM—GAMBLE Class

DMS—DORSEY Class

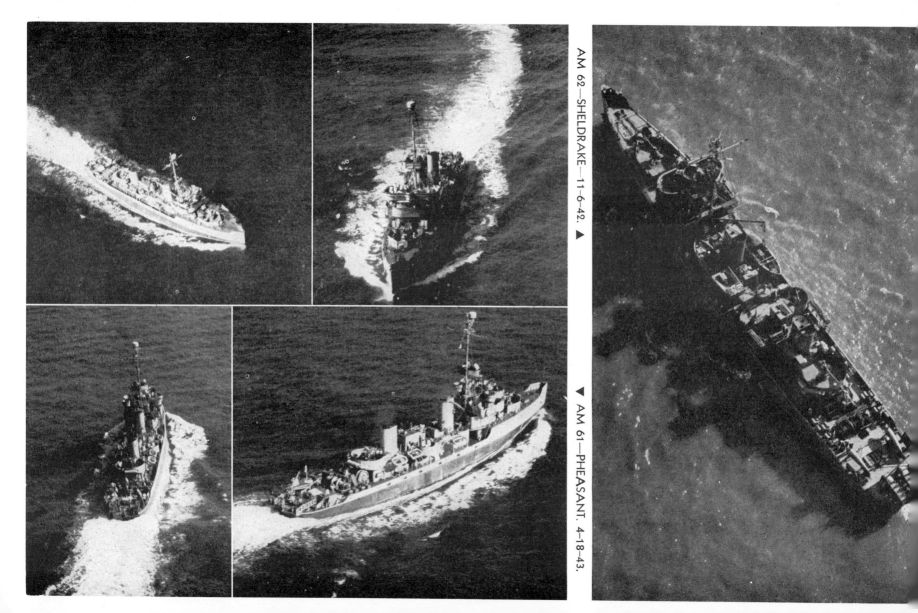

AM 62—SHELDRAKE—11-6-42. ▶

▼ AM 61—PHEASANT. 4-18-43.

FLEET MINESWEEPERS—AM

The 220-foot, steel hulled, AUK Class Sweepers (improved RAVEN design) provide the fleet with fast mine sweeper/layers readily adaptable to various patrol details, including convoy escort over long distances. Standard displacement is 890 tons. The British AM-100 Class is of this type. Other AM classes include the ADMIRABLE Class, a PCE variation; the 173-foot ADROIT Class, a coverted PC design; 2 World War I 187-foot BIRD Class types; and some of the larger steel-hulled converted trawlers, also used as YP's.

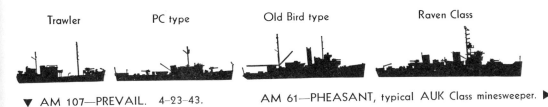

Trawler PC type Old Bird type Raven Class

▼ AM 107—PREVAIL. 4-23-43.   AM 61—PHEASANT, typical AUK Class minesweeper. ▶

MOTOR MINESWEEPERS—YMS

An extremely large group; these 260-ton, 135-foot, wooden-hulled vessels are equipped to deal with all types of mines. Both types are furnished to the United Kingdom through lend-lease. One unit has been converted to YDG (degaussing vessel).

SUBCHASER—PCS

▼ The 136-foot PCS uses a YMS hull with a PCE-type superstructure; or with an extended superstructure is employed as a rescue craft.

YMS

▲ Early design has 2 stacks, rounded pilot houses; later, and most numerous type, has 1 stack, squared pilot house, flared bow and other minor differences.

YMS • YDG

▼ Some units of this design have been converted during construction to perform YMS functions.

PCS • YMS

AT · ARS · ASR

New construction in the minor ship classifications is represented by the vessels shown here; steel-hulled craft designed and built by the Navy. These include AT—Oceangoing tug; ARS—Salvage Vessels; and ASR—Submarine Rescue Vessels.

The new type of 1,600 ton ARS, exemplified by ARS—34 GEAR. Wooden-hull sisterships are lend-leased. ▼

▲ ASR 9—FLORICAN.

▲ The new 1,500 ton Fleet Tug design—NAVAJO Class.

▼ One unit serves as an ASR. Latest units have no stack. ▼ CREE shows original design.

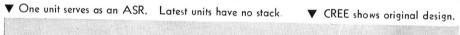

▼ A unit of the new 2,000-ton ASR CHANTICLEER Class.

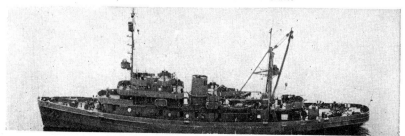

▲ Typical rig as Salvage Vessel, as Seaplane Tender (small). ▼

Completed during and after World War I as the 54 BIRD Class minesweepers—these ships have been diverted with slight modifications to the above uses. Two are retained in their original function.

▼ SANDPIPER—AVP 9, a small Seaplane Tender.

▲ Two other functions served by this type are as buoy tender and sub rescue craft.

YP—DISTRICT PATROL CRAFT

▲ YP 429, 96 feet o. a.

▼ YP 222, 75 feet o. a.

▲ YP 275, ex-SEGELEN, 107 feet o. a.

▼ YP 600, 78 feet o. a.

YP's include a great many miscellaneous fishing craft and other small vessels now serving as armed outpost and patrol boats. Similar craft are also found in the Coast Guard, Army, and in the Navy as AM—Mine craft, AG—Miscellaneous auxiliaries, PYc—Coastal Yachts, YDG—Degaussing Vessels, and IX—Unclassified vessels. Typical vessels are illustrated.

Many are now being laid up or returned to their owners.

▲ AM 66—BULLFINCH, 136 feet o. a.

▼ YP 515, 157 feet o. a.

▲ YP 21, 75 feet o. a.

▼ YP 422, 147 feet o. a.

COASTAL SMALL CRAFT

Hundreds of small craft of many sizes and types have been pressed into service by the Navy and Coast Guard and used for coastal patrol and other important, strictly local assignments. The vessels shown here indicate only a few of the types now in such service.

▲ ARS—RESCUER, typical of many Army and Navy conversions of coastal freighters and bulk cargo carriers.

▲ Tuna fishermen converted to AMc—Coastal minesweepers.
▼ A large new class is the APc—Coastal Transport.

ATR—Rescue tugs, are typical of a large fleet of new and converted small craft used as AT, AG, and in USCG reserve. ▶

This particular design constitutes a large class in both the U. S. and British Navies.

HARBOR CRAFT

A complete list of the 42 types and their designations appears in ONI 54–I. Some of the commercial and Coast Guard types are illustrated in 54–A and 54–CG. The vessels shown here are only a few of the many types used for harbor operations and defense and are representative of some of the large classes of ships.

▲ A unit of the Army's GENERAL Class mine-planters.

▼ ARS 13—ANCHOR, one of a large new class. Several have been lend-leased to the U. K.

▲ A new USMC type YW—Water-barge.

▼ A harbor-defense net-tender of the 152' TREE Class. The 194' AILANTHUS Class is building. Note typical bow design for net handling.

INDEX BY TYPES

ESCORT VESSELS—DE

EVARTS Class (Short Hull)

DE	5	EVARTS
DE	6	WYFELS
DE	7	GRISWOLD
DE	8	STEELE
DE	9	CARLSON
DE	10	BEBAS
DE	11	CROUTER
DE	13	BRENNAN
DE	14	DOHERTY
DE	15	AUSTIN
DE	16	EDGAR G. CHASE
DE	17	EDWARD C. DALY
DE	18	GILMORE
DE	19	BURDEN R. HASTINGS
DE	20	LE HARDY
DE	21	HAROLD C. THOMAS
DE	22	WILEMAN
DE	23	CHARLES R. GREER
DE	24	WHITMAN
DE	25	WINTLE
DE	26	DEMPSEY
DE	27	DUFFY
DE	28	EMERY
DE	29	STADTFELD
DE	30	MARTIN
DE	31	SEDERSTROM
DE	32	FLEMING
DE	33	TISDALE
DE	34	EISELE
DE	35	FAIR
DE	36	MANLOVE
DE	37	GREINER
DE	38	WYMAN
DE	39	LOVERING
DE	40	SANDERS
DE	41	BRACKETT
DE	42	REYNOLDS
DE	43	MITCHELL
DE	44	DONALDSON
DE	45	ANDRES
DE	47	DECKER
DE	48	DOBLER
DE	49	DONEFF
DE	50	ENGSTROM
DE	256	SEID
DE	257	SMARTT
DE	258	WALTER S. BROWN
DE	259	WILLIAM C. MILLER
DE	260	CABANA
DE	261	DIONNE
DE	262	CANFIELD
DE	263	DEEDE
DE	264	ELDEN
DE	265	CLOUES
DE	301	LAKE
DE	302	LYMAN
DE	303	CROWLEY
DE	304	RALL
DE	305	HALLORAN
DE	306	CONNOLLY
DE	307	FINNEGAN
DE	308	CREAMER
DE	309	ELY
DE	310	DELBERT W. HALSEY
DE	311	KEPPLER
DE	312	LLOYD THOMAS
DE	313	WILLIAM C. LAWE
DE	314	WILLARD KEITH
DE	315	
DE	527	O'TOOLE
DE	528	JOHN J. POWERS
DE	529	MASON
DE	530	JOHN M. BERMINGHAM

BUCKLEY Class (Long Hull)

DE	51	BUCKLEY
DE	53	CHARLES LAWRENCE
DE	54	DANIEL T. GRIFFIN
DE	56	DONNELL
DE	57	FOGG
DE	59	FOSS
DE	60	GANTNER
DE	62	GEORGE W. INGRAM
DE	63	IRA JEFFREY
DE	65	LEE FOX
DE	66	AMESBURY
DE	68	BATES
DE	69	BLESSMAN
DE	70	JOSEPH E. CAMPBELL
DE	99	CANNON
DE	100	CHRISTOPHER
DE	101	ALGER
DE	102	THOMAS
DE	103	BOSTWICK
DE	104	BREEMAN
DE	105	BURROWS
DE	112	
DE	113	
DE	129	EDSALL
DE	130	JACOB JONES
DE	131	HAMMANN
DE	132	ROBERT E. PEARY
DE	133	PILLSBURY
DE	134	POPE
DE	135	FLAHERTY
DE	136	FREDERICK C. DAVIS
DE	137	HERBERT C. JONES
DE	138	DOUGLAS L. HOWARD
DE	139	FARQUHAR
DE	140	J. R. Y. BLAKELY
DE	141	HILL
DE	142	FESSENDEN
DE	143	FISKE
DE	144	FROST
DE	145	HUSE
DE	146	INCH
DE	147	BLAIR
DE	148	BROUGH
DE	149	CHATELAIN
DE	150	MEUNZER
DE	151	POOLE
DE	152	PETERSON
DE	153	REUBEN JAMES
DE	154	SIMS
DE	155	HOPPING
DE	156	REEVES
DE	157	FECHTELER
DE	158	CHASE
DE	159	LANING
DE	160	LOY
DE	161	BARBER
DE	162	LEVY
DE	163	McCONNELL
DE	164	OSTERHAUS
DE	165	PARKS
DE	166	BARON
DE	167	ACREE
DE	168	AMICK
DE	169	ATHERTON
DE	170	BOOTH
DE	171	CARROLL
DE	172	COONER
DE	173	ELDRIDGE
DE	174	MARTS
DE	175	PENNEWILL
DE	176	MICKA
DE	177	REYBOLD
DE	178	HERZOG
DE	179	McANN
DE	180	TRUMPETER
DE	181	STRAUB
DE	182	GUSTAFSON
DE	183	MILES
DE	184	WESSON
DE	185	RIDDLE
DE	186	SWEARER
DE	187	STERN
DE	188	O'NEILL
DE	189	BRONSTEIN
DE	190	BAKER
DE	191	COFFMAN
DE	192	EISNER
DE	193	GARFIELD THOMAS
DE	194	WINGFIELD
DE	195	THORNHILL

DE 196 RINEHART	DE 238 STEWART	DE 329 KRETCHMER	DE 404 EVERSALE
DE 197 ROCKE	DE 239 STRUTEVANT	DE 330 O'REILLY	DE 405 DENNIS
DE 198 LOVELACE	DE 240 MOORE	DE 331 KOINER	DE 406 EDMONDS
DE 199 MANNING	DE 241 KEITH	DE 332 PRICE	DE 407 SHELTON
DE 200 NUENDORF	DE 242 TOMICH	DE 333 STRICKLAND	DE 408 STRAUS
DE 201 JAMES E. CRAIG	DE 243 J. RICHARD WARD	DE 334 FORSTER	DE 409 LA PRADE
DE 202 EICHENBERGER	DE 244 OTTERSTETTER	DE 335 DANIEL	DE 410 JACK MILLER
DE 203 THOMASON	DE 245 SLOAT	DE 336 ROY O. HALE	DE 411 STAFFORD
DE 204 JORDAN	DE 246 SNOWDEN	DE 337 DALE W. PETERSON	DE 412 through 426. Unassigned
DE 205 NEWMAN	DE 247 STANTON	DE 338 MARTIN H. RAY	DE 438 CORBESIER
DE 206 LIDDLE	DE 248 SWASEY	DE 339 JOHN C. BUTLER	DE 439 CONKLIN
DE 207 KEPHART	DE 249 MARCHAND	DE 340 O'FLAHERTY	DE 440 McCOY REYNOLDS
DE 208 COFER	DE 250 HURST	DE 341 RAYMOND	DE 441 WILLIAM SEIVERLING
DE 209 LLOYD	DE 251 CAMP	DE 342 RICHARD W. SUESENS	DE 442 ULVERT M. MOORE
DE 210 OTTER	DE 252 HOWARD D. CROW	DE 343 ABERCROMBIE	DE 443 through 454
DE 211 HUBBARD	DE 253 PETTIT	DE 344 OBERRENDER	DE 508 GILLIGAN
DE 212 HAYTER	DE 254 RICKETTS	DE 345 ROBERT BRAZIER	DE 509 FORMOE
DE 213 WILLIAM T. POWELL	DE 255 SELLSTROM	DE 346 EDWIN A. HOWARD	DE 510 through 515. Unassigned
DE 214 SCOTT	DE 281 ARTHUR L. BRISTOL	DE 347 JESSE RUTHERFORD	DE 531 EDWARD H. ALLEN
DE 215 BURKE	DE 282 TRUXTON	DE 348 through 381. Unassigned	DE 532 TWEEDY
DE 216 ENRIGHT	DE 283 UPHAM	DE 382 RAMSDEN	DE 533 HOWARD F. CLARK
DE 217 COOLBAUGH	DE 284 VOGELGESANG	DE 383 MILLS	DE 534 SILVERSTEIN
DE 218 DARBY	DE 285 WEEKS	DE 384 RHODES	DE 535 LEWIS
DE 219 J. DOUGLAS BLACKWOOD	DE 286 SUTTON	DE 385 RICHEY	DE 536 BIVIN
DE 220 FRANCIS M. ROBINSON	DE 287 WILLIAM M. WOOD	DE 386 SAVAGE	DE 537 RIZZI
DE 221 SOLAR	DE 288 WILLIAM R. RUSH	DE 387 VANCE	DE 538 OSBERG
DE 222 FOWLER	DE 289	DE 388 LANSING	DE 539 WAGNER
DE 223 SPANGENBERG	DE 290 WILLIAMS	DE 389 DURANT	DE 540 VANDIVIER
DE 224 RUDDEROW	DE 291 through 300. Unassigned	DE 390 CALCATERRA	DE 541 SHEEHAN
DE 225 DAY	DE 316 HARVESON	DE 391 CHAMBERS	DE 542 OSWALD A. POWERS
DE 226 CROSLEY	DE 317 JOYCE	DE 392 MERRILL	DE 543 GROVES
DE 227 CREAD	DE 318 KIRKPATRICK	DE 393 HAVERFIELD	DE 544 ALFRED WOLF
DE 228	DE 319 LEOPOLD	DE 394 SWENNING	DE 545 HAROLD J. ELLISON
DE 229	DE 320 MENGES	DE 395 WILLIS	DE 546 MYLES C. FOX
DE 230 CHAFFEE	DE 321 MOSLEY	DE 396 JANSSEN	DE 547 CHARLES R. WARE
DE 231 HODGES	DE 322 NEWELL	DE 397 WILHOITE	DE 548 CARPELLOTTI
DE 232 KINZER	DE 323 PRIDE	DE 398 COCKRILL	DE 549 EUGENE A. GREENE
DE 233 REGISTER	DE 324 FALGOUT	DE 399 STOCKDALE	DE 550 GYATT
DE 234 BROCK	DE 325 LOWE	DE 400 HISSEM	DE 551 through 562. Unassigned
DE 235 JOHN Q. ROBERTS	DE 326 GARY	DE 401 HOLDER	DE 575 AHRENS
DE 236 WILLIAM M. HOBBY	DE 327 BRISTER	DE 402 RICHARD S. BULL	DE 576 BARR
DE 237 RAY K. EDWARDS	DE 328 FINCH	DE 403 RICHARD M. ROWELL	DE 577 ALEXANDER J. LUKE

INDEX BY TYPES

DE 578 ROBERT I. PAINE
DE 579 RILEY
DE 580 LESLIE L. B. KNOX
DE 581 McNULTY
DE 582 through 614. Unassigned
DE 633 FOREMAN
DE 634 WHITEHURST
DE 635 ENGLAND
DE 636 WITTER
DE 637 BOWERS
DE 638 WILLMARTH
DE 639 GENDREAU
DE 640 FIEBERLING
DE 641 WILLIAM C. COLE
DE 642 PAUL G. BAKER
DE 643 DAMON M. CUMMINGS
DE 644 VAMMEN
DE 665 JENKS
DE 666 DURIK
DE 667 WISEMAN
DE 668 YOKES
DE 669 PAVLIC
DE 670 ODUN
DE 671 JACK C. ROBINSON
DE 672 BASSETT
DE 673 JOHN P. GRAY
DE 674 JOSEPH M. AUMAN
DE 675 WEBER
DE 676 SCHMITT
DE 677 FRAMENT
DE 678 HARMON
DE 679 GREENWOOD
DE 680 LOESER
DE 681 GILLETTE
DE 682 UNDERHILL
DE 683 HENRY R. KENYON
DE 684 DELONG
DE 685 COATES
DE 686 EUGENE E. ELMORE
DE 687 through 692. Unassigned
DE 693 BULL
DE 694 BUNCH

DE 695 RICH
DE 696 SPANGLER
DE 697 GEORGE
DE 698 RABY
DE 699 MARSH
DE 700 CURRIER
DE 701 OSMUS
DE 702 EARL V. JOHNSON
DE 703 HOLTON
DE 704 CRONIN
DE 705 FRYBARGER
DE 706 through 714. Unassigned
DE 721
DE 739 BANGUST
DE 740 WATERMAN
DE 741 WEAVER
DE 742 HILBERT
DE 743 LAMONS
DE 744 KYNE
DE 745 SNYDER
DE 746 HEMMINGER
DE 747 BRIGHT
DE 748 TILLS
DE 749 ROBERTS
DE 750 McCLELLAND
DE 751 GAYNIER
DE 752 CURTIS W. HOWARD
DE 753 JOHN J. VAN BUREN
DE 763 CATES
DE 764 GANDY
DE 765 EARL K. OLSEN
DE 766 SLATER
DE 767 OSWALD
DE 768 EBERT
DE 769
DE 770
DE 789 TATUM
DE 790 BORUM
DE 791 MALOY
DE 792 HAINES
DE 793 RUNELS
DE 794 HOLLIS

DE 795 GUNASON
DE 796 MAJOR
DE 797 WEEDEN
DE 798 VARIAN
DE 799 SCROGGINS
DE 800 JACK W. WILKE

FRIGATES—PF

ASHEVILLE Class

PF 1 ASHEVILLE
PF 2 NATCHEZ

TACOMA Class

PF 3 TACOMA
PF 4 SAUSALITO
PF 5 HOQUIAM
PF 6 PASCO
PF 7 ALBUQUERQUE
PF 8 EVERETT
PF 9 POCATELLO
PF 10 BROWNSVILLE
PF 11 GRAND FORKS
PF 12 CASPER
PF 13 PUEBLO
PF 14 GRAND ISLAND
PF 15 ANNAPOLIS
PF 16 BANGOR
PF 17 KEY WEST
PF 18 ALEXANDRIA
PF 19 HURON
PF 20 GULFPORT
PF 21 BAYONNE
PF 22 GLOUCESTER
PF 23 SHREVEPORT
PF 24 MUSKEGON
PF 25 CHARLOTTSVILLE
PF 26 POUGHKEEPSIE
PF 27 NEWPORT
PF 28 EMPORIA
PF 29 GROTON
PF 30 HINGHAM
PF 31 GRAND RAPIDS

PF 32 WOONSOCKET
PF 33 DEARBORN
PF 34 LONGBEACH
PF 35 BELFAST
PF 36 GLENDALE
PF 37 SAN PEDRO
PF 38 CORONADO
PF 39 OGDEN
PF 40 EUGENE
PF 41 EL PASO
PF 42 VAN BUREN
PF 43 ORANGE
PF 44 CORPUS CHRISTI
PF 45 HUTCHINSON
PF 46 BISBEE
PF 47 GALLUP
PF 48 ROCKFORD
PF 49 MUSCOGEE
PF 50 CARSON CITY
PF 51 BURLINGTON
PF 52 ALLENTOWN
PF 53 MACHIAS
PF 54 SANDUSKY
PF 55 BATH
PF 56 COVINGTON
PF 57 SHEBOYGAN
PF 58 BRIDGEPORT
PF 59 BEAUFORT
PF 60 CHARLOTTE
PF 61 MANITOWOC
PF 62 WORCESTER
PF 63 SCRANTON
PF 64 KNOXVILLE
PF 65 CHATTANOOGA
PF 66 READING
PF 67 PEORIA
PF 68 BRUNSWICK
PF 69 DAVENPORT
PF 70 EVANSVILLE
PF 71 NEW BEDFORD
PF 93 ROANOKE
PF 94 SITKA

PF 95 STAMFORD
PF 96 MACON
PF 97 LORAIN
PF 98 MILLEDGEVILLE
PF 99 ORLANDO
PF 100 RACINE
PF 101 GREENSBORO
PF 102 FORSYTH

EAGLE BOATS-PE

PE 19, 27, 32, 38, 48, 55–57

GUNBOATS-PG

PG 17 DUBUQUE
PG 18 PADUCAH
PG 19 SACRAMENTO
PG 22 TULSA
PG 51 CHARLESTON
PG 53 VIXEN
PG 54 ST. AUGUSTINE
PG 56 WILLIAMSBURG
PG 59 SAN BERNARDINO
PG 60 BEAUMONT
PG 61 DAUNTLESS
PG 72 NOURMAHAL

TEMPTRESS Class

PG 62 TEMPTRESS
PG 63 SURPRISE
PG 64 SPRY
PG 65 SAUCY
PG 66 RESTLESS
PG 67 READY
PG 68 IMPULSE
PG 69 FURY
PG 70 COURAGE
PG 71 TENACITY
PG 86 ACTION
PG 87 ALACRITY
PG 89 BRISK

PG 92 HASTE
PG 93 INTENSITY
PG 94 MIGHT
PG 95 PERT
PG 96 PRUDENT

YACHTS-PY

PY 10 ISABEL
PY 12 SYLPH
PY 13 SIREN
PY 14 ARGUS
PY 16 ZIRCON
PY 18 TURQUOISE
PY 19 CARNELIAN
PY 20 TOURMALINE
PY 21 RUBY
PY 22 AZURLITE
PY 23 BERYL
PY 24 ALMANDITE
PY 25 CRYSTAL
PY 27 GIRASOL
PY 28 MARCASITE
PY 29 MIZPAH
PY 31 CYTHERA
PY 32 SOUTHERN SEAS

COASTAL YACHTS-PYc

PYc 1 EMERALD
PYc 2 SAPPHIRE
PYc 3 AMETHYST
PYc 4 AGATE
PYc 5 ONYX
PYc 6 AMBER
PYc 7 AQUAMARINE
PYc 10 TOPAZ
PYc 11 ANDRADITE
PYc 12 SARDONYX
PYc 13 JASPER
PYc 15 GARNET
PYc 16 CHALCEDONY

PYc 17 PYROPE
PYc 18 PERIDOT
PYc 19 RHODOLITE
PYc 20 JET
PYc 21 ALABASTER
PYc 22 OLIVIN
PYc 25 PHENAKITE
PYc 26 CYMOPHANE
PYc 27 COLLEEN
PYc 28 ABILITY
PYc 29 GALLANT
PYc 31 LASH
PYc 36 PARAGON
PYc 37 MENTOR
PYc 38 CAROLITA
PYc 39 MARNELL
PYc 40 CAPTOR
PYc 41 IOLITE
PYc 42 LEADER
PYc 43 SEA SCOUT
PYc 44 PERSEVERANCE
PYc 45 BLACK DOUGLAS
PYc 46 IMPETUOUS
PYc 47 PATRIOT
PYc 48 PERSISTENT
PYc 49 RETORT
PYc 50 STURDY
PYc 51 VALIANT
PYc 52 VENTURE

SUBMARINE CHASERS PC

PC 451 Class (Experimental Boats)

PC 451
PC 452

PC 461 Class

PC 461–466
PC 469–495
PC 542
PC 543, 545, 546

PC 548–603, 606
PC 608–621, 623–627
PC 776–825
PC 1077–1088
PC 1119–1149
PC 1167–1235, 1237–1247
PC 1251–1265
PC 1546–1559, 1563–1569

PATROL VESSELS– ESCORT-PCE

PCE 842–847
PCE 867–886
PCE 891–904

PATROL CRAFT ESCORT-RESCUE-PCE(R)

PCE(R) 848–866

PATROL VESSELS— SUBMARINE CHASERS PCS

136′ Class

PCS 1376–1392
PCS 1396, 1397
PCS 1402–1405
PCS 1413, 1414
PCS 1417–1426
PCS 1429–1431
PCS 1441, 1442
PCS 1445, 1446
PCS 1449–1452
PCS 1455
PCS 1457–1461
PCS 1464, 1465

INDEX BY TYPES

SUBMARINE CHASERS
SC

110' Class

SC 102
SC 330
SC 412
SC 431
SC 432
SC 437
SC 449
SC 450

111' Class

SC 453
SC 497
SC 498
SC 499
SC 500
SC 502–508
SC 511–522
SC 524–541
SC 628–693
SC 695
SC 697–708
SC 710–718
SC 722–739
SC 741–750
SC 752–761
SC 768–775
SC 977–1023
SC 1025–1062
SC 1064–1072
SC 1266–1282
SC 1290–1334
SC 1338–1343
SC 1347–1375
SC 1474–1493
SC 1496–1499
SC 1502–1508
SC 1510–1512
SC 1517

FAIRMILE TYPE

SC 1467, 1468, 1472, 1473

MOTOR GUNBOATS–PGM

PGM 1–8 (ex SC's)

MOTOR TORPEDO BOATS
PT

PT 20 Class

PT 20, 24, 27, 29, 30
PT 36
PT 38–40
PT 42
PT 45–48
PT 59–66

PT 71 Class (78')

PT 71–84
PT 199–313
PT 450–485

PT 95 Class (78')

PT 95–102

PT 103 Class (80')

PT 103–196
PT 314–367
PT 485–563

MOTOR TORPEDO BOATS
(SUBMARINE CHASERS)
PTC

(63' Type)
PTC 37–66

MINE LAYERS–CM

CM 5   TERROR
CM 8   KEOKUK (now AKN)
CM 9   MONADNOCK
CM 10   MIANTONOMAH
CM 11   SALEM
CM 12   WEEHAWKEN
CMc 3   WASSUC

LIGHT MINE LAYERS
DM

GAMBLE Class

DM 15   GAMBLE
DM 16   RAMSAY
DM 17   MONTGOMERY
DM 18   BREESE
DM 19   TRACY
DM 20   PREBLE
DM 21   SICARD
DM 22   PRUITT

MINE SWEEPERS, HIGH SPEED–DMS

DORSEY Class

DMS 1   DORSEY
DMS 2   LAMBERTON
DMS 3   BOGGS
DMS 4   ELLIOT
DMS 5   PALMER
DMS 6   HOGAN
DMS 7   HOWARD
DMS 8   STANSBURY
DMS 9   CHANDLER
DMS 10   SOUTHARD
DMS 11   HOVEY
DMS 12   LONG
DMS 13   HOPKINS
DMS 14   ZANE
DMS 16   TREVER
DMS 17   PERRY
DMS 18   HAMILTON

MINE SWEEPERS–AM

"BIRD" Class (Old)

AM 21   LARK
AM 35   WHIPPOORWILL

RAVEN Class (220')

AM 55   RAVEN
AM 56   OSPREY

AUK Class (220')

AM 57   AUK
AM 58   BROADBILL
AM 59   CHICKADEE
AM 60   NUTHATCH
AM 61   PHEASANT
AM 62   SHELDRAKE
AM 63   SKYLARK
AM 64   STARLING
AM 65   SWALLOW

CONVERTED TRAWLERS

AM 66   BULLFINCH
AM 67   CARDINAL
AM 68   CATBIRD
AM 69   CURLEW
AM 70   FLICKER
AM 71   ALBATROSS
AM 72   BLUEBIRD
AM 73   GRACKLE
AM 74   GULL
AM 75   KITE
AM 76   LINNET
AM 77   GOLDFINCH
AM 79   GOSHAWK
AM 80   GOLDCREST
AM 81   CHAFFINCH
AM 133   HAWK
AM 134   IBIS
AM 135   MERGANSER

ADROIT Class (173')

AM 82 ADROIT
AM 83 ADVENT
AM 84 ANNOY
AM 85 CONFLICT
AM 86 CONSTANT
AM 87 DARING
AM 88 DASH
AM 89 DESPITE
AM 90 DIRECT
AM 91 DYNAMIC
AM 92 EFFECTIVE
AM 93 ENGAGE
AM 94 EXCEL
AM 95 EXPLOIT
AM 96 FIDELITY
AM 97 FIERCE
AM 98 FIRM
AM 99 FORCE

HEED Class (221')

AM 100 HEED
AM 101 HERALD
AM 102 MOTIVE
AM 103 ORACLE
AM 104 PILOT
AM 105 PIONEER
AM 106 PORTENT
AM 107 PREVAIL
AM 108 PURSUIT
AM 109 REQUISITE
AM 110 REVENGE
AM 111 SAGE
AM 112 SEER
AM 114 STAFF
AM 116 SPEED
AM 117 STRIVE
AM 118 STEADY
AM 119 SUSTAIN
AM 120 SWAY
AM 121 SWERVE
AM 122 SWIFT

AM 123 SYMBOL
AM 124 THREAT
AM 125 TIDE
AM 126 TOKEN
AM 127 TUMULT
AM 128 VELOCITY
AM 131 ZEAL
AM 314 CHAMPION
AM 315 CHIEF
AM 316 COMPETENT
AM 317 DEFENSE
AM 318 DEVASTATOR
AM 319 GLADIATOR
AM 320 IMPECCABLE
AM 322 SPEAR
AM 323 TRIUMPH
AM 324 VIGILANCE
AM 340 ARDENT
AM 341 DEXTROUS

ADMIRABLE Class (185')

AM 136 ADMIRABLE
AM 137 ADOPT
AM 148 ASTUTE
AM 149 AUGURY
AM 150 BARRIER
AM 151 BOMBARD
AM 152 BOND
AM 153 BUOYANT
AM 154 CANDID
AM 155 CAPABLE
AM 156 CAPTIVATE
AM 157 CARAVAN
AM 158 CAUTION
AM 159 CHANGE
AM 160 CLAMOUR
AM 161 CLIMAX
AM 162 COMPEL
AM 163 CONCISE
AM 164 CONTROL
AM 165 COUNSEL
AM 214 CRAIG

AM 215 CRUISE
AM 216 DEFT
AM 217 DELEGATE
AM 218 DENSITY
AM 219 DESIGN
AM 220 DEVICE
AM 221 DIPLOMA
AM 222 DISDAIN
AM 223 DOUR
AM 224 EAGER
AM 225 ELUSIVE
AM 226 EMBATTLE
AM 227 EMBROIL
AM 228 ENHANCE
AM 229 EQUITY
AM 232 EXECUTE
AM 233 FACILITY
AM 234 FANCY
AM 235 FIXITY
AM 238 GARLAND
AM 239 GAYETY
AM 240 HAZARD
AM 246 IMPLICIT
AM 247 IMPROVE
AM 248 INCESSANT
AM 249 INCREDIBLE
AM 250 INDICATIVE
AM 251 INFLICT
AM 252 INSTILL
AM 253 INTRIGUE
AM 254 INVADE
AM 255 JUBILANT
AM 256 KNAVE
AM 257 LANCE
AM 258 LOGIC
AM 259 LUCID
AM 260 MAGNET
AM 261 MAINSTAY
AM 262 MARVEL
AM 263 MEASURE
AM 264 METHOD
AM 265 MIRTH

AM 266 NIMBLE
AM 267 NOTABLE
AM 268 NUCLEUS
AM 269 OPPONENT
AM 270 PALISADE
AM 271 PENETRATE
AM 272 PERIL
AM 273 PHANTOM
AM 274 PINNACLE
AM 275 PIRATE
AM 276 PIVOT
AM 277 PLEDGE
AM 278 PROJECT
AM 279 PRIME
AM 280 PROWESS
AM 283 RANSOM
AM 284 REBEL
AM 285 RECRUIT
AM 286 REFORM
AM 287 REFRESH
AM 288 REIGN
AM 294 SALUTE
AM 295 SAUNTER
AM 296 SCOUT
AM 297 SCRIMMAGE
AM 298 SCUFFLE
AM 299 SENTRY
AM 300 SERENE
AM 301 SHELTER
AM 302 SIGNET
AM 303 SKIRMISH
AM 304 SKURRY
AM 305 SPECTACLE
AM 306 SPECTOR
AM 307 STAUNCH
AM 308 STRATEGY
AM 309 STRENGTH
AM 310 SUCCESS

INDEX BY TYPES

MOTOR MINESWEEPERS
YMS

YMS 1–132
YMS 134–136
YMS 138–140
YMS 143–147
YMS 151
YMS 158–160
YMS 163–166
YMS 169–170
YMS 176–180
YMS 183–184
YMS 192–193
YMS 195–201
YMS 207–208
YMS 215–216
YMS 218–220
YMS 222
YMS 224
YMS 226–228
YMS 231
YMS 235
YMS 237–239
YMS 241–243
YMS 247–251
YMS 259–260
YMS 262–263
YMS 265–276
YMS 281
YMS 283
YMS 285–343
YMS 345–445
YMS 446–481 (PCS Type)

HARBOR MINESWEEPERS
AMb

AMb 1   ELIZABETH

COASTAL MINESWEEPERS
AMc

AMc   1   PIPIT
AMc   2   MAGPIE
AMc   3   PLOVER
AMc   5   KESTREL
AMc   6   HEATH HEN
AMc   8   COCKATOO
AMc   9   CROSSBILL
AMc 10   LONGSPUR
AMc 11   SANDERLING
AMc 12   GROUSE
AMc 14   CONDOR
AMc 15   WAXBILL
AMc 16   CHATTERER
AMc 17   PINTAIL
AMc 20   CROW
AMc 21   KILDEER
AMc 22   FLAMINGO
AMc 24   EGRET
AMc 25   CANARY
AMc 26   HUMMINGBIRD
AMc 27   FRIGATE BIRD
AMc 28   MOCKING BIRD
AMc 29   PUFFIN
AMc 30   REEDBIRD
AMc 32   COURSER
AMc 33   FIRECREST
AMc 34   PARRAKEET
AMc 35   ROADRUNNER

ACCENTOR Class

AMc 36   ACCENTOR
AMc 37   BATELEUR
AMc 38   BARBET
AMc 39   BRAMBLING
AMc 40   CARACARA
AMc 41   CHARCALACA
AMc 42   CHIMANGO
AMc 43   COTINGA
AMc 44   COURLAN

AMc 45   DEVELIN
AMc 46   FULMAR
AMc 47   JACAMAR
AMc 48   LIMPKIN
AMc 49   LORIKEET
AMc 50   MARABOUT
AMc 51   OSTRICH
AMc 52   ROLLER
AMc 53   SKIMMER
AMc 54   TAPACOLA
AMc 55   TURACO
AMc 56   KINGBIRD
AMc 57   PHOEBE
AMc 58   RHEA
AMc 59   RUFF

ACME Class

AMc 61   ACME
AMc 62   ADAMANT
AMc 63   ADVANCE
AMc 64   AGGRESSOR
AMc 65   ASSERTIVE
AMc 66   AVENGE
AMc 67   BOLD
AMc 68   BULWARK
AMc 69   COMBAT
AMc 70   CONQUEROR
AMc 71   CONQUEST
AMc 72   COURIER
AMc 73   DEFIANCE
AMc 74   DEMAND
AMc 75   DETECTOR
AMc 76   DOMINANT
AMc 77   ENDURANCE
AMc 82   GOVERNOR
AMc 83   GUIDE
AMc 84   HEROIC
AMc 85   IDEAL
AMc 86   INDUSTRY
AMc 87   LIBERATOR
AMc 88   LOYALTY
AMc 89   MEMORABLE

AMc 90   MERIT
AMc 91   OBSERVER
AMc 92   PARAMOUNT
AMc 93   PEERLESS
AMc 94   PLUCK
AMc 95   POSITIVE
AMc 96   POWER
AMc 97   PRESTIGE
AMc 98   PROGRESS
AMc 99   RADIANT
AMc 100   RELIABLE
AMc 101   ROCKET
AMc 102   ROYAL
AMc 103   SECURITY
AMc 104   SKIPPER
AMc 105   STALWART
AMc 106   SUMMIT
AMc 107   TRIDENT
AMc 108   VALOR
AMc 109   VICTOR
AMc 110   VIGOR
AMc 111   AGILE
AMc 112   AFFRAY
AMc 149   NIGHTINGALE

MISCELLANEOUS AUXILIARIES—AG

(Most of these are illustrated in 54-A)

AG   1   HANNIBAL
AG 12   GOLD STAR
AG 16   UTAH
AG 17   WYOMING
AG 23   SEQUOIA
AG 24   SEMMES
AG 25   POTOMAC
AG 29   BEAR
AG 31   ARGONNE
AG 33   KAULA
AG 41   PANAY

CAMANGA Class

AG 42 CAMANGA
AG 66 BESBORO
AG 45 TAGANAK
AG 46 TULURAN
AG 44 MALANAO
AG 49 ANACAPA
AG 50 KOPARA
AG 67 ANTAEUS

MOTOR TORPEDO BOAT TENDERS–AGP

AGP 2 HILO
AGP 3 JAMESTOWN

LST TYPE

AGP 4 PORTUNUS
AGP 5 VARUNA
AGP 10 ORESTES
AGP 11 SILENUS

AVP Type

AGP 6 OYSTER BAY
AGP 7 MOBJACK
AGP 8 WACHAPREAGUE
AGP 9 WILLOUGHBY

USMC Type

AGP 12 ACONTIUS
AGP 13 CYRENE

SURVEYING SHIPS–AGS

AGS 1 PATHFINDER
AGS 2 HYDROGRAPHER
AGS 3 OCEANOGRAPHER
AGS 4 BOWDITCH
AGS 5 SUMNER

COASTAL TRANSPORTS APc

APc 1–50
APc 86–96
APc 101–103
APc 108–111

HIGH SPEED TRANSPORTS (Destroyer Type)–APD

MANLEY CLASS

APD 1 MANLEY
APD 6 STRINGHAM
APD 7 TALBOT
APD 8 WATERS
APD 9 DENT
APD 10 BROOKS
APD 11 GILMER
APD 12 HUMPHREYS
APD 13 SANDS
APD 14 SCHLEY
APD 15 KILTY
APD 16 WARD
APD 17 CROSBY
APD 18 KANE
APD 19 TATTNALL
APD 20 ROPER
APD 21 DICKERSON
APD 22 HERBERT
APD 23 OVERTON
APD 24 NOA

SALVAGE VESSELS–ARS

OLD "BIRD" Class

ARS 1 VIKING
ARS 2 CRUSADER
ARS 3 DISCOVERER
ARS 11 WARBLER
ARS 12 WILLET

DIVER Class

ARS 5 DIVER
ARS 6 ESCAPE
ARS 7 GRAPPLE
ARS 8 PRESERVER
ARS 9 SHACKLE
ARS 16 EXTRICATE
ARS 17 RESTORER
ARS 18 RESCUER
ARS 19 CABLE
ARS 20 CHAIN
ARS 21 CURB
ARS 22 CURRENT
ARS 23 DELIVER
ARS 24 GRASP
ARS 25 SAFEGUARD
ARS 26 SEIZE
ARS 27 SNATCH
ARS 28 VALVE
ARS 29 VENT
ARS 30 ACCELERATE
ARS 31 HARJURAND
ARS 32 BRANT
ARS 33 CLAMP
ARS 34 GEAR
ARS 35 WEIGHT
ARS 36 SWIVEL
ARS 37 TACKLE

ANCHOR Class

ARS 13 ANCHOR
ARS 14 PROTECTOR
ARS 15 EXTRACTOR

SUBMARINE RESCUE VESSELS–ASR

OLD "BIRD" Class

ASR 1 WIDGEON
ASR 2 FALCON
ASR 3 CHEWINK
ASR 4 MALLARD
ASR 5 ORTOLAN

CHANTICLEER Class

ASR 7 CHANTICLEER
ASR 8 COUCAL
ASR 9 FLORICAN
ASR 10 GREENLET
ASR 11 MACAW
ASR 12 PENGUIN

OCEAN-GOING TUGS–AT

185' Class

AT 12 SONOMA
AT 13 ONTARIO

157' Class

AT 19 ALLEGHENY
AT 20 SAGAMORE
AT 21 BAGADUCE
AT 23 KALMIA
AT 24 KEWAYDIN
AT 25 UMPQUA
AT 26 WANDANK
AT 27 TATNUCK
AT 28 SUNNADIN
AT 29 MAHOPAC
AT 30 SCIOTA
AT 33 PINOLA
AT 34 ALGORMA
AT 37 IUKA
AT 38 KEOSANQUA
AT 39 MONTCALM
AT 58 UNDAUNTED
AT 63 ACUSHNET

NAVAJO Class (205')

AT 66 CHEROKEE
AT 67 APACHE
AT 68 ARAPAHO
AT 69 CHIPPEWA
AT 70 CHOCTAW
AT 71 HOPI

INDEX BY TYPES

AT 72 KIOWA
AT 73 MENOMINEE
AT 74 PAWNEE
AT 75 SIOUX
AT 76 UTE
AT 81 BANNOCK
AT 82 CARIB
AT 83 CHICKASAW
AT 84 CREE
AT 85 LIPAN
AT 86 MATACO
AT 87 MORENO
AT 88 NARRAGANSETT
AT 90 PINTO
AT 91 SENECA
AT 92 TAWASA
AT 93 TEKESTA
AT 94 YUMA
AT 95 ZUNI
AT 96 ABNAKI
AT 97 ALSEA
AT 98 ARIKARA
AT 100 CHOWANOC
AT 101 COCOPA
AT 102 HIDATSA
AT 103 HITCHITI
AT 104 JICARILLA
AT 105 MOCTOBI
AT 106 MOLALA
AT 107 MUNSEE
AT 108 PAKANA
AT 109 POTAWATOMI
AT 110 QUAPAW
AT 111 SARSI
AT 112 SERRANO
AT 113 TAKELMA
AT 114 TAWAKONI
AT 115 TENINO
AT 116 TOLOWA
AT 117 WATEREE
AT 118 WENATCHEE

OLD "BIRD" Class

AT 131 BOBOLINK
AT 133 CORMORANT
AT 135 KINGFISHER
AT 136 ORIOLE
AT 137 OWL
AT 138 PARTRIDGE
AT 139 RAIL
AT 140 ROBIN
AT 141 SEAGULL
AT 142 TERN
AT 143 TURKEY
AT 144 VIREO
AT 145 WOODCOCK
AT 147 ESSELEN
AT 166 CHETCO
AT 167 CHATOT

RESCUE TUGS–ATR

165' Class

ATR 1–16
ATR 21–40
ATR 50–89

143' Class

ATR 43–47
ATR 90
ATR 97–140

SEAPLANE TENDERS (Destroyer Type)–AVD

CHILDS Class

AVD 1 CHILDS
AVD 7 WILLIAM B. PRESTON
AVD 10 BALLARD
AVD 11 THORNTON
AVD 12 GILLIS

SEAPLANE TENDERS (Small)–AVP

LAPWING Class (Old "Bird" Class)

AVP 1 LAPWING
AVP 2 HERON
AVP 3 THRUSH
AVP 4 AVOCET
AVP 5 TEAL
AVP 6 PELICAN
AVP 7 SWAN
AVP 9 SANDPIPER

BARNEGAT Class

AVP 10 BARNEGAT
AVP 11 BISCAYNE
AVP 12 CASCO
AVP 13 MACKINAC
AVP 21 HUMBOLDT
AVP 22 MATAGORDA
AVP 23 ABSECON
AVP 24 CHINCOTEAGUE
AVP 25 COOS BAY
AVP 26 HALF MOON
AVP 29 ROCKAWAY
AVP 30 SAN PABLO
AVP 31 UNIMAK
AVP 32 YAKUTAT
AVP 33 BARATARIA
AVP 34 BERING STRAIT
AVP 35 CASTLE ROCK
AVP 36 COOK INLET
AVP 37 CORSON
AVP 38 DUXBURY BAY
AVP 39 GARDINER'S BAY
AVP 40 FLOYD'S BAY
AVP 41 GREENWICH BAY
AVP 48 ONSLOW
AVP 49 ORCA
AVP 50 REHOBOTH
AVP 51 SAN CARLOS
AVP 52 SHELIKOF
AVP 53 SUISUN
AVP 54 TIMBALIER
AVP 55 VALCOUR

UNCLASSIFIED–IX

IX 2 DESPATCH
IX 8 CUMBERLAND
IX 13 HARTFORD
IX 15 PRAIRIE STATE
IX 20 CONSTELLATION
IX 21 CONSTITUTION
IX 25 REINA MERCEDES
IX 29 WILMETTE
IX 30 DOVER
IX 33 NEWTON
IX 39 SEATTLE
IX 40 OLYMPIA
IX 41 AMERICA
IX 42 CAMDEN
IX 43 FREEDOM
IX 45 FAVORITE
IX 46 TRANSFER
IX 47 VAMARIE
IX 48 HIGHLAND LIGHT
IX 49 SPINDRIFT
IX 50 BOWDOIN
IX 52 CHENG HO
IX 54 GALAXY
IX 57 ARANER
IX 58 DWYN WEN
IX 60 SEAWARD
IX 62 VILEEHI
IX 64 WOLVERINE
IX 65 BLUE DOLPHIN
IX 66 MIGRANT
IX 67 GUINEVERE
X 68 SEVEN SEAS
IX 71 KAILUA
IX 72 LIBERTY BELLE
IX 73 ZACA
IX 74 METHA NELSON
IX 75 JOHN M. HOWARD

IX 76	RAMONA
IX 77	JUNIATA
IX 78	BRAVE
IX 79	EL CANO
IX 81	SABLE
IX 82	LUSTER
IX 83	ASHLEY
IX 84	CONGAREE
IX 85	EUNAW
IX 86	POCOTALIGO
IX 87	SALUDA
IX 88	WIMBEE
IX 89	ROMAIN
IX 91	PALOMAS
IX 92	LISTON
IX 93	IRENE FORSYTE
IX 95	ECHO
IX 97	MARTHA'S VINEYARD
IX 98	MOOSEHEAD
IX 99	SEA CLOUD
IX 100	RACER
IX 101	BIG CHIEF
IX 102	MAJABA
IX 103	E. A. POE
IX 104	P. H. BURNETT
IX 105	PANTHER
IX 106	GREYHOUND
IX 107	ZEBRA
IX 108	ATLANTIDA
IX 109	ANTELOPE
IX 110	OCELOT
IX 111–130	ARMADILLO Class (see 54-A)
IX 131	ABARENDA
IX 132	ANDREW DORIA
IX 133	ANTONA
IX 134	ARAYAT
IX 135	ARETHUSA
IX 136	CARONDELET
IX 137	CELTIC
IX 138	MALVERN
IX 139	OCTORARA

IX 140	QUIROS
IX 141	MANILENO
IX 142	SIGNAL
IX 143	SILVER CLOUD
IX 144	ST. MARY
IX 145	VILLALOBOS

DEGAUSSING VESSELS YDG

YDG 1–3	(exYP'S)
YDG 5	
YDG 6	(exYMS)

MOTOR TUGS–YMT

65' Class
YMT 1–5, 8–12, 23

Miscellaneous
YMT 14, 15, 17, 19–22, 24–29

NET TENDERS–YN

TREE Class (152')

YN 1	ALOE
YN 2	ASH
YN 3	BOXWOOD
YN 4	BUTTERNUT
YN 5	CATALPA
YN 6	CHESTNUT
YN 7	CINCHONA
YN 8	BUCKEYE
YN 9	BUCKTHORN
YN 10	EBONY
YN 11	EUCALYPTUS
YN 12	CHINQUAPIN
YN 13	GUM TREE
YN 14	HOLLY
YN 15	ELDER
YN 16	LARCH
YN 17	LOCUST
YN 18	MAHOGANY
YN 19	MANGO

YN 20	HACKBERRY
YN 21	MIMOSA
YN 22	MULBERRY
YN 23	PALM
YN 24	HAZEL
YN 25	REDWOOD
YN 26	ROSEWOOD
YN 27	SANDALWOOD
YN 28	NUTMEG
YN 29	TEABERRY
YN 30	TEAK
YN 31	PEPPERWOOD
YN 32	YEW

IMPROVED TREE Class (194')

YN 57	AILANTHUS
YN 58	BITTERBUSH
YN 59	ANAQUA
YN 60	BARETTA
YN 61	CLIFFROSE
YN 62	SATINLEAF
YN 63	CORKWOOD
YN 64	CORNEL
YN 65	MASTIC
YN 66	CANOTIA
YN 67	LANCEWOOD
YN 68	PAPAYA
YN 69	ROYAL PALM
YN 70	SILVERBELL
YN 71	SNOWBALL
YN 72	SPICEWOOD
YN 73	MANCHINEEL
YN 74	TORCHWOOD
YN 75	WINTERBERRY
YN 76	VIBURNUM
YN 77	ABELE
YN 78	BALM
YN 81	CATCLAW
YN 82	CHINABERRY
YN 83	HOPTREE
YN 84	WHITEWOOD
YN 85	PALO BLANCO

YN 86	PALOVERDE
YN 87	PINON
YN 91	SHELLBARK
YN 92	SILVERLEAF
YN 93	STAGBUSH
YN 94	ALLTHORN
YN 95	TESOTA
YN 96	YAUPON
YN 97–121	

GATE VESSELS–YNG

110' Class
YNG 1–18
YNG 22–30
YNG 40–41

Miscellaneous
YNG 19–21
YNG 31–39
YNG 42, 43

NET TENDERS–Tug Class

YNT 1	HOPOCAN
YNT 2	MENEWA
YNT 3	ONEKA
YNT 4	MAHASKA
YNT 5	KESHENA
YNT 6	CANASATEGO
YNT 7	DONACONA
YNT 8	MANKATO
YNT 9	METEA
YNT 10	OKISKO
YNT 11	TAHCHEE
YNT 12	TAMAHA
YNT 13	WAPASHA
YNT 14	NAMONTACK
YNT 15	COCKENOE
YNT 16	KATLIAN
YNT 17	NESWAGE
YNT 18	ANNAWAN
YNT 19	METACOM
YNT 20	TAMAQUE

INDEX BY TYPES

YNT 21   MARIN
YNT 22   NOKA
YNT 23   NAWAT
YNT 24   WAPELLO
YNT 25   ADARIO

DISTRICT PATROL VESSELS–YP

YP 4–9
YP 11, 12
YP 14, 15
YP 19–25
YP 27–29
YP 31–46
YP 48–64
YP 66, 67
YP 69, 70, 73
YP 75, 76
YP 78–92
YP 94–96
YP 99–109, 112, 114, 117, 120
YP 131–133, 137, 138, 142, 144, 146
YP 148, 149, 151–157
YP 159–161
YP 163–166, 168, 170, 175
YP 179–181, 184

YP 187–189, 191–192
YP 197, 199
YP 202–204
YP 208–223, 225
YP 227–229
YP 231–234
YP 236–253
YP 255–257
YP 259, 260
YP 262–264
YP 267–268
YP 271–273, 275, 278
YP 280–283
YP 285–293, 295
YP 297–302
YP 304–308
YP 311–313, 315
YP 317, 318, 322
YP 327–329
YP 331–334
YP 337–340, 342
YP 347–359
YP 362–365
YP 369–371
YP 373–386, 388
YP 390–395
YP 398–403

YP 406–428
YP 430–437
YP 441–443, 445
YP 447–450, 452
YP 454–480
YP 482–491
YP 493–503
YP 505–521, 523
YP 525–527
YP 529–534, 536, 537
YP 541–543
YP 546–554
YP 556–559
YP 563–566
YP 568–570
YP 572–574
YP 578–595
YP 597, 598
YP 600–615

HARBOR TUGS–YT

Miscellaneous

YT 2–9
YT 16–18, 24
YT 32, 34, 36, 39, 42
YT 112, 115, 119–126

YT 128, 132, 135, 136
YT 170, 171, 173, 187, 213
YT 238–240, 242, 243, 252, 271
YT 322–326, 329, 332–337, 341–363
YT 360, 362, 364–366, 460, 462
YT 464–466

100′ Class

YT 133–134, 138–142, 145–151, 174–182
YT 188–195
YT 265–276, 327, 328, 331, 338
YT 364–421, 458, 459, 463

66′ Class

YT 132, 143, 144, 152–169
YT 184–186
YT 196–212
YT 230–237
YT 244–251
YT 291–321
YT 339, 340
YT 422–457, 461

110′ Class

YT 215–229
YT 253–264
YT 277–290

U. S. NAVAL AUXILIARIES

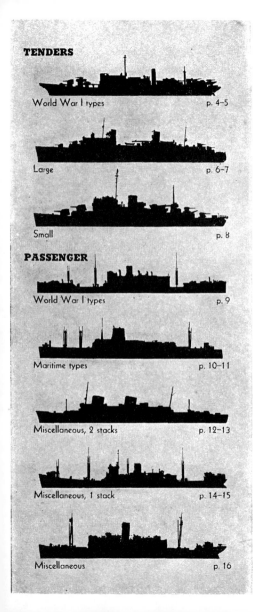

TENDERS

World War I types   p. 4–5

Large   p. 6–7

Small   p. 8

PASSENGER

World War I types   p. 9

Maritime types   p. 10–11

Miscellaneous, 2 stacks   p. 12–13

Miscellaneous, 1 stack   p. 14–15

Miscellaneous   p. 16

U. S. FLEET TRAIN—

AD Destroyer Tenders   Page

2	MELVILLE	28
3, 4	DOBBIN Class	4
9	BLACK HAWK	28
11, 12	ALTAIR Class	28
14, 15, 17–19	DIXIE Class	7
16	CASCADE	10
20, 21	HAMUL Class	22

AE Ammunition Ships

1, 2	PYRO Class	4
3–9	LASSEN Class	21
10	SANGAY	26
11, 12	MT. HOOD Class	19

AF Provision Storeships

1	BRIDGE	5
7–9	ARCTIC Class	17
10	ALDEBARAN	19
11	POLARIS	18
12, 13, 15, 17, 21, 22	MIZAR Class	16
14	URANUS	29
16, 18	PASTORES Class	16
19	ROAMER	27
20	PONTIAC	27
23, 25	CYGNUS Class	28
24	DELPHINUS	28
26	OCTANS	16
27	PICTOR	28
28, 29	HYADES Class	20

AG Miscellaneous Auxiliaries

1	HANNIBAL	29
12	GOLD STAR	17
29	BEAR	29
31	ARGONNE	9
33	KAULA	35
42, 45, 46, 66	CAMANGA Class	29
44	MALANAO	35
67	ANTEAUS	16

AGC Combined Operations—Communications Headquarters Ship

1–3, 5	APPALACHIAN Class	19
4	ANCON	11

AGP Motor Torpedo Boat Tenders

6–9	OYSTER BAY Class	8

AGS Surveying Ships   (See also 54–MC)   Page

4	BOWDITCH	14
5	SUMNER	29

AH Hospital Ships

1	RELIEF	5
5	SOLACE	16
6–8	COMFORT Class	26
9	BOUNTIFUL	5
10	SAMARITAN	9
11	REFUGE	9

AK Cargo Ships

13, 15–17	CAPELLA Class	17
14	REGULUS	17
41	HERCULES	25
42, 43	MERCURY Class	19
46	PLEIADES	27
47	AQUILA	27
48	PEGASUS	27
49	SATURN	27
51	ARIES	17
63	ASTERION	
70–79, 90–97, 99–	CRATER Class	25
80	ENCELADUS	35
98	AURIGA	26
156–		35

AKA Attack Cargo Ships

1, 6–8, 11	ARCTURUS Class	18
2–4, 12–14	PROCYON Class	21
5	FOMALHAUT	26
9	ALHENA	26
10	ALMAACK	25
15–20, 53–63	ANDROMEDA Class	19
21–52		10
64–87		19

AKN Net Cargo Ships

1–3	INDUS Class	25

AKS General Stores Issue Ships

1	CASTOR	19
3	ANTARES	17
4	POLLUX	20
5–9	ACUBENS Class	25

AKV Cargo Ship—Aircraft Ferry

1, 2	KITTY HAWK Class	35

LARGE AUXILIARIES

AO Oilers		Page
3, 4	CUYAMA Class	31
2	MAUMEE	31
9, 11–13, 18–21	PATOKA Class	31
15–17	KAWEAH Class	31
22–32, 51–64	CIMARRON Class	32
34, 35	CHICOPEE Class	33
36–40, 48, 68, 70, 71	KENNEBEC Class	32
41–44, 47	MATTAPONI Class	33
46	VICTORIA	34
49, 50, 65, 67, 73–88	PECOS-SUAMICO Class	33
66	ATASCOSA	34
69, 72	ENOREE Class	34

AOG (YO) Gasoline Tankers		
1–11, 48–59	PATAPSCO Class	36
17–46, 60, 61	METTAWEE Class	36

AP Troop Transports		
6	W. W. BURROWS	14
7	WHARTON	9
21, 22	WAKEFIELD Class	12
23	WEST POINT	13
24	ORIZABA	13
29	U. S. GRANT	14
33	REPUBLIC	14
41	STRATFORD	14
54, 61	HERMITAGE Class	13
63	ROCHAMBEAU	12
67	DOROTHEA L. DIX	25
69, 70, 76	ELIZ. STANTON Class	23
71	LYON	22
72	SUSAN B. ANTHONY	15
75	GEMINI	17
77	THURSTON	20
103, 104	"PRESIDENT" Class	10
106, 107	CATSKILL Class	30
110–119	"GENERAL" Class	10
120–129	"ADMIRAL" Class	10
130–159	GEN. SQUIER Class	36
162–165	KENMORE Class	25

APA Attack Transports		
1, 11	DOYEN Class	30
2, 3, 12, 14–17	HARRIS Class	9
5	BARNETT	15
6–9	HEYWOOD Class	15
10	HARRY LEE	14

		Page
13	J. T. DICKMAN	9
18–20, 30	PRESIDENT Class	10
21, 28, 31, 32	CRESCENT CITY Class	11
25–27	A. MIDDLETON Class	11
33–48, 92, 93, 95, 96, 99–102, 104	BAYFIELD Class	24
49–51, 94,	ORMSBY Class	20
52–56, 91, 97, 98, 103, 105	SUMTER Class	24
57–88		10
89, 90	FUNSTON Class	26

APH Wounded Evacuation Transports		
1–3	TRYON Class	25

AR Repair Ships		
1	MEDUSA	5
3, 4	PROMETHEUS Class	28
5–7	VULCAN Class	7
9, 12	DELTA Class	22
10	ALCOR	14
11	RIGEL	28

ARG Repair Ship—Internal Combustion Engine		
2–11	LUZON Class	25

ARH Hull Repair Ships		
1	JASON	7

AS Submarine Tenders		
3	HOLLAND	5
5	BEAVER	16
11, 12, 15–19	FULTON Class	7
13, 14, 23–26	GRIFFIN Class	22
20	OTUS	26
22	EURYALE	23

AV Seaplane Tenders		
1	WRIGHT	9
4, 5	CURTISS Class	6
8	TANGIER	23
9, 10	POCOMOKE Class	23

AVP Seaplane Tenders, Small		
10–55	BARNEGAT Class	8

IX Unclassified (See also 54–MC)		
102	MAJABA	29
111–130	ARMADILLO Class	25

SMT Special Military Types		
1–	MARINE Class	36
YO–YOG	Miscellaneous	35

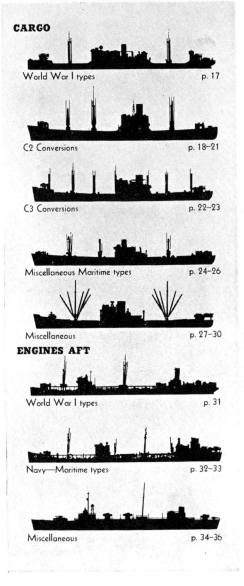

CARGO

World War I types — p. 17

C2 Conversions — p. 18–21

C3 Conversions — p. 22–23

Miscellaneous Maritime types — p. 24–26

Miscellaneous — p. 27–30

ENGINES AFT

World War I types — p. 31

Navy—Maritime types — p. 32–33

Miscellaneous — p. 34–36

WORLD WAR I TENDERS—AD • AR • AS • AE • AF • AH

The first Navy-built Train; originally one design. Formed the basis of the peacetime tender fleet.

DOBBIN Class—AD 3, 4 ▲ WHITNEY 4/17/42

PYRO Class—AE 1, 2 ▼ PYRO

▼ HOLLAND—AS 3-4/22/43

RELIEF—AH 1 ▼   BOUNTIFUL—AH9, Similar

MEDUSA—AR1 – 2/15/43

▼ BRIDGE—AF 1 – 8/8/42

LARGE TENDERS — AD • AR • AS • AV

Based on one general design and adapted to fulfill each specific Train function

CURTISS Class—AV 4, 5, all photos ALBEMARLE–4/43–6/10/43

FULTON Class—AS 11, 12, 15–19 ▼ SPERRY–7/24/42

DIXIE Class—AD 14, 15, 17–19 ▼ PRAIRIE

VULCAN Class—AR 5–7 (ARH 1 similar) ▼ VULCAN–6/10/42

SMALL TENDERS—AVP • AGP

A multipurpose design employed as seaplane and small craft tenders, and in escort and patrol duties.   Note the variation in aircraft-handling facilities and armament

BARNEGAT Class—AVP 10–55 ▲ SAN PABLO ▼ AVP 22   Below right—AGP 6, OYSTER BAY

▼ ARGONNE Class—AG 31, AH 10—USSB "HOG ISLAND"ers, AH 11 similar (silhouette)
Sister ships ST. MIHIEL, CHATEAU THIERRY (ex-AP 31, 32) SOMME, and CAMBRAI are Army-operated

▼ J. T. DICKMAN—4/8/43

▼ WRIGHT—AV 1 – 7/13/43 converted from "HOG ISLAND 448" type

⬍ WHARTON Class—AP 7, APA 13   A variation of the HARRIS Class

▼ HARRIS Class—APA 2, 3, 12, 14–17   USSB "STATE" type

PASSENGER—MARITIME COMMISSION TYPES—AP • APA • AD • AGC

▼ "PRESIDENT" Class—APA 18–20, 30, AP 103, 104, C3–P & C Type

New types still building—

"ADMIRAL" Class—
    AP 120–129

S4–SE2–BDI Type—
    APA 57–88
    AKA 21–52

"GENERAL" Class—AP 110–119 P2–S2–R2 design▼   CASCADE–AD 16 – 4/28/43 ▶

▼ CRESCENT CITY Class—APA 21, 28, 31, 32, P & C type, former Delta Liners   ▼ CALVERT—12/24/42

▲ CHARLES CARROLL—5/6/43   ARTHUR MIDDLETON ▼

▲ ARTHUR MIDDLETON Class—APA 25-27, AGC 4, USAT PARKER, C3-P & C type, former American-S. Africa and Panama Lines   ▼ GEORGE CLYMER—9/1/42

PASSENGER—MISCELLANEOUS TWO-STACKERS—AP

▼ ROCHAMBEAU—AP 63 – 10/5/42, ex-MARECHAL JOFFRE. The Japanese operate a sister ship.

WAKEFIELD Class—AP 21, 22, ex-MANHATTAN, WASHINGTON   ▼ WAKEFIELD—5/11/42

▼ HERMITAGE Class—AP 54, 61, ex-Italian CONTE BIANCAMANO, CONTE GRANDE—sister ship CONTE VERDE is Japanese controlled

▼ WEST POINT—AP 23 – 6/43, ex-AMERICA

▼ ORIZABA—AP 24 – 11/17/42, Former NY & Cuba Mail Line; sister ship USAT SIBONEY

PASSENGER—MISCELLANEOUS ONE-STACKERS—AP • APA • AGS • AR

▼ STRATFORD—AP 41 – 5/4/42. U. S. Shipping Board "Laker"

▼ BOWDITCH—AGS 4 – 12/28/42   W. W. BURROWS—AP 6 similar

▼ REPUBLIC—AP 33

▼ ALCOR—AR 10–preconversion

▼ HARRY LEE—APA 10. Formerly American Export Liner–5/14/43

▼ U. S. GRANT—AP 29, with REPUBLIC served as peacetime Army transports

SUSAN B. ANTHONY Class—AP 72, APA 5 (ex-Grace Liners) ▼ SUSAN B. ANTHONY 9/14/42

▼ NEVILLE—2/19/43   HEYWOOD Class—APA 6–9, ex-Baltimore Mail "City" type . ▼ HEYWOOD

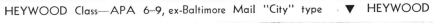

PASSENGER—MISCELLANY—AF • AS • AH • AG

▼ MIZAR Class—AF 12, 13, 15, 17, 21, 22. Formerly United Fruit ships ▼

▼ ANTEAUS—AG 67–6/25/43   Sister ships include
SOLACE—AH 5, and 2 others under Army control

▼ BEAVER—AS 5–4/7/42

▼ TALAMANCA–6/30/42   ▲ MERAK–6/23/43

▼ PASTORES Class—AF 16, 18, OCTANS AF 26, similar with another passenger deck

CAPELLA Class—AK 13, 15-17, AKS 3, AG 12, USSB "HOG ISLAND"ers. ▼ VEGA-9/8/42

Silhouette shows original appearance
retained by merchant sister ships

◄ ARCTIC Class—AF 7-9-6/6/43

REGULUS—AK 14-3/20/42 ▶

◄ ARIES—AK 51-5/26/42

GEMINI—AP 75, USSB "Lake" type ▶
USCG operate sister ships.

ARCTURUS Class—AKA 1, 6-8, 11, AF 11   ▼ BETELGEUSE-4/10/43

C2-Cargo type. Original appearance, typical of merchant sister ships, is silhouetted.   ▼ ALCYONE-5/15/43

MERCURY Class—AK 42, 43, AKS 1, AF 10   C2–Cargo type   ▼   ALDEBARAN—9/28/42   C2–S–AJ1 type similar—AE 11, 12, AKA 64–87

APPALACHIAN Class—AGC 1–3, 5
C-2 SB 1 Conversion   ▼

◄ ANDROMEDA Class—AKA 15–20, 53–63
ANDROMEDA—4/18/43   C2–SB1 type
The reinforced trestle masts, designed
for lowering loaded landing craft, will
replace the goalposts on most AKAs.

Silhouette illustrates the original design
of these conversions.

CARGO—C-2 CONVERSIONS—AP · APA · AKA · AKS · AE · AF

ORMSBY Class—AP 77, APA 49–51, 94, AKS 4, AF 28, 29   C2F–Cargo type

▲ THURSTON–9/23/42

◄ ORMSBY–7/18/43

APA94–BAXTER similar with lowered kingposts for'd.
AF 28, 29–HYADES Class similar with single kingposts.
Both types are C2–SE1 designs.

Original design of ships shown on this
and page 21 is silhouetted above.

◄ POLLUX–6/19/43

PROCYON-LASSEN Class—AKA 2-4, 12-14, AE 3-9   C2F-Cargo   ▼ PROCYON-5/10/43   Kingposts are to be replaced with trestle masts on AKA's

▼ RAINIER-6/20/43

▼ ELECTRA-7/3/43

CARGO—C-3 CONVERSIONS—AD • AP • AR • AS • AV

HAMUL Class—AD 20, 21　▼　MARKAB-10/7/42

Compare these ships (all C-3) with merchant sister ships shown silhouetted

GRIFFIN Class—AS 13, 14, 23-26, AP 71 (silhouette)　▼　GRIFFIN　　▼　DELTA Class—AR 9, 12　BRIAREUS—AR 12, has goalpost in place of crane

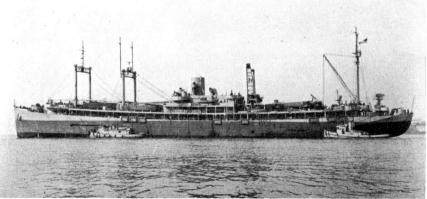

POCOMOKE Class—AV 9, 10 ▼ POCOMOKE—2/3/43

▼ TANGIER—AV 8–9/2/42   EURYALE—AS 22 similar without crane.   ELIZ. STANTON Class—AP 69, 70, 76 ▼ ARUNDEL—5/1/43

BAYFIELD Class—
APA 33–48, 92, 93, 95, 96, 99–102, 104   C3–SA2 type   ▲ CUSTER–7/24/43

SUMTER Class—
APA 52–56, 91, 97, 98, 103, 105   C3–SA3 type   ▼ WINDSOR–6/27/43

HERCULES Class AK 41, AKA 10, AP 67   C3E Cargo type   ▼ ALMAACK—10/15/43   Silhouette shows AK, AP sister ships

TRYON Class—APH 1-3   C2-S1-A1 type   ▼ PINKNEY—1/1/43

CRATER Class—AK 70-79, 90-97, 99—, AKN 1-3, AKS 5-9, AP 162-165, IX 111-130, ARG 2-11   EC2-SC1 or "Liberty" type   ▼ ALUDRA—1/6/43

CARGO—MISCELLANEOUS M. C. TYPES—AE • AH • AK • AKA • AS

FUNSTON Class—APA 89, 90   C3–S1–A3 type   ▼ J. O'HARA–5/1/43

◄ OTUS—AS 20 – 1/15/43
   C1B type   AH 6–8 similar

AURIGA—AK 98–4/1/43   C1B type ►

◄ S A N G A Y Class—AE 10,
   AKA 5   C1A Cargo

ALHENA—AKA 9   C-2 Cargo ►

▼ PLEIADES—AK 46–3/18/43

▲ ROAMER—AF 19

▲ PEGASUS—AK 48

ACQUILA—AK 47–8/4/42 ▶

▼ PONTIAC—AF 20–6/9/42

SATURN—AK 49–8/5/42 ▲

CARGO—MISCELLANEOUS OLD TYPES—AD · AF · AR · AG · AGS · IX

ALTAIR Class—AD 11, 12, AR 11 ▼ DENEBOLA–3/11/43   COMPOSITE SUPERSTRUCTURE   PROMETHEUS Class—AR 3, 4 ▼ VESTAL

▼ MELVILLE—AD 2–12/28/43   SPLIT SUPERSTRUCTURE   CYGNUS Class—AF 23, 25 ▼ TAURUS–11/30/42

▼ BLACK HAWK—AD 9   ▼ DELPHINIUS—AF 24–9/6/42   PICTOR—AF 27 similar

▼ SUMNER—AGS 5

◄ BEAR—AG 29—3/16/43

▲ URANUS (Preconversion)—AF 14

▲ HANNIBAL—AG 1

BESBORO ▲
MAJABA—IX 102 similar

CAMANGA Class—AG
42, 45, 46, 66

▼ TAGANAK—7/26/42

CARGO—SPECIAL CONVERSIONS

DOYEN Class—APA 1, 11—all photos DOYEN-6/7/43   P1–S2–L2 Design   CATSKILL Class—AP 106, 107 similar

PATOKA Class—AO 9, 11–13, 18–21 "Flush-deckers" ▼ RAMAPO—4/17/43   Minor superstructure variations occur   The first Train oilers built to Navy specifications

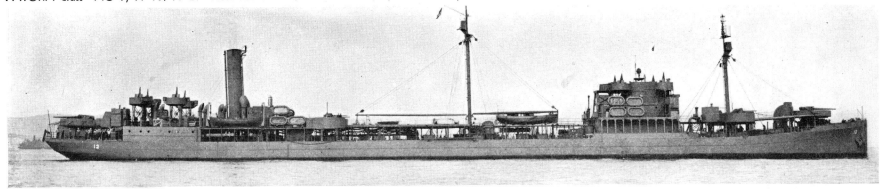

CUYAMA Class—AO 3, 4

KAWEAH Class—AO 15, 16 ▼ LARAMIE—2/21/43

▼ MAUMEE—AO 2–7/22/42

TANKERS—NAVY—MARITIME COMMISSION TYPES

CIMARRON Class—AO 22–32   Improved CIMARRON Class, AO 51–64—similar   Note armament, king post variations   ▼   SALAMONIE—10/18/42

▲ SABINE AO 25—7/28/42   KENNEBEC Class—AO 36–40, 48, 68, 70, 71   ▼ WINOOSKI—10/15/42   Maritime Commission T2 type   ▲ NIOBRARA—4/14/43

TANKERS—NAVY—MARITIME COMMISSION TYPES

PECOS–SUAMICO Class—AO49, 50, 65, 67, 73–88

Maritime Commission T2–SE–A1 type ▼

▲ SAUGATUCK–6/21/43

MATTAPONI Class—AO 41–44, 47   USMC "TANKER" type   ▲ MONONGAHELA–9/24/42

CHICOPEE Class—AO 34, 35
▼ HOUSATONIC 10/21/42

MISCELLANEOUS TANKERS

▼ ATASCOSA—AO 66-3/14/43

ENOREE Class—AO 69, 72

Special reinforced 160-ton tower and boom has been added to KENNEBEC Class oilers for unloading LCT 5 or 6 from the deck of LSTs.

▼ BIG HORN—Now in Coast Guard

VICTORIA—AO 46 ▶

AK · AKV · AG · YO · YOG   MISCELLANEOUS "ENGINES—AFT"

KITTY HAWK Class—AKV 1, 2   ▼ HAMMONDSPORT   Army operated   LAKEHURST similar

▼ KAULA—AG 33–4/21/43   ▲ YO, YOG—Concrete type

AK 156 Class—C1–M–AVI Design
Coastal Cargo Carrier

AK 80—ENCELADUS
Army and British Sisterships

▲ MALANAO—AG 44–7/28/42

MISCELLANEOUS "ENGINES—AFT" AP • AOG • SMT

▼ GENERAL SQUIER Class—AP 130–159   USMC C4–S–A1 type

▼ MARINE Class—SMTI—USMC C4–SBI design

▼ PATAPSCO Class—AOG 1–11, 48–59   ▲ METTAWEE Class—AOG 17–46, 60,

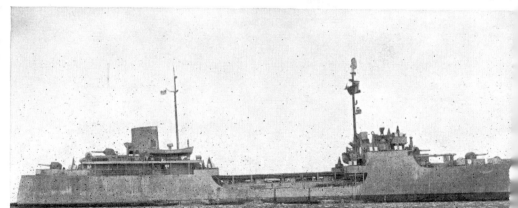

U. S. LANDING CRAFT

U. S. LANDING CRAFT

LST—Landing Ship for Tanks—Length o. a.—327'9".

The largest of our "beaching" units, these ocean-going vessels are often seen carrying LCT or other equipment as deck cargo. Tanks are landed through bow gates after beaching. Often, in order to reach inaccessible points, float extensions are employed. Recent models carry 6-LCP on davits, heavier AA armament.

Variations of this design are the ARB—Battle Damage Repair Ship; ARL—Auxiliary Repair Ship; AGP—Auxiliary Motor Torpedo Boat Tender.

LCI—Landing Craft for Infantry.

Length o. a.—158'4".

These ships represent one of the larger troop-landing types used by the United Nations. Troops are disembarked over extended ramps on either side of the bow. At distances they might be mistaken for submarines.

There are now two types in operation—

Nos. 1–350, shown on this page, is the older design no longer in production. Its bridge has recently been heightened as illustrated.

No. 351– varies in deckhouse, interior arrangement, and armament, as illustrated at the right.

LCT–Mk V

LCT–Mk V, VI—Landing Craft for Tanks.
Length o. a.—112' (Mark V left), 105' (Mark VI below).

These medium tank-landing craft are often seen transported on LST's or in sections on APA's and AKA's. They are the largest of the U. S. open-deck, bow-ramp types. Note the low, barge-like appearance and the wide wake, characteristics of these and smaller craft.

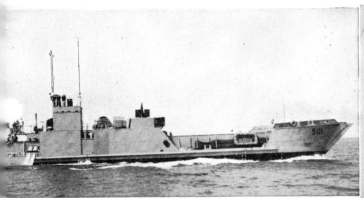

LCV—Landing Craft for Vehicles. **LCVP**—Landing Craft Vehicles, personnel. Length o. a.—36'4''.

Used as both vehicle and personnel carriers **LCVP**, these and LCM's are transported and operated from APA's and AKA's.   LCV ▼   LCVP ▶

LCM—Landing Craft for Mechanized Equipment.   Length o. a.—50'-56'. These units may carry one tank or assorted vehicles and cargo.   They are distinguished from the LCV and LCT by their grilled bow ramp.

LCS—Support Landing Craft.

Length o. a.—36'.

These craft are employed to provide firepower support in landing operations. Note similarity to the LCC.

LCC—Control Landing Craft.

Length o. a.—56'.

The tall antennae and masts illustrated fold down during high-speed maneuvers.

LCP—Personnel Landing Craft.

Length o. a.—36'.

This and the bow-ramp version (LCPR) are the standard assault boats. They are often seen being transported on AP's, AK's, and APD's, or as illustrated, towing a fleet of LCR's (Rubber landing rafts).

▼ LCS ▶

▼ LCP   ▲ LCPR   ▲ LCP towing LCR's.   ▼ LCP

VEHICLES

The amphibious LVT (tracked landing vehicle) shown below is used as both a cargo and personnel carrier. This type has proven effective in landing operations involving reefs, swamps, etc.

◀ Two and one-half ton amphibian truck (Duck) capable of transporting mechanized equipment by tandem method. ▼

▼ LVT(2)—Tracked landing vehicle, unarmored.   ▼ LVT(A)1—Tracked landing vehicle, armored.   ▼ Amphibian "Jeep" (¼-ton truck).

LSD—Landing Ship, Dock.
Length o. a.—457'9''.

Designed to transport and launch LCT's and LCM's, this ship is an adaptation of the floating dry-dock.

U. S. COAST GUARD VESSELS

COAST GUARD CUTTERS

PATROL CRAFT

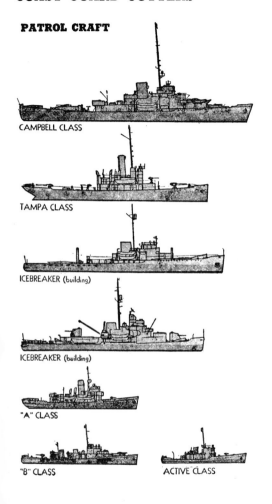

CAMPBELL CLASS

TAMPA CLASS

ICEBREAKER (building)

ICEBREAKER (building)

"A" CLASS

"B" CLASS   ACTIVE CLASS

TENDERS

CACTUS—IRONWOOD—IRIS CLASSES

MISCELLANEOUS CUTTERS

MOTORBOATS

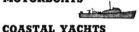

COASTAL YACHTS

EX-FISHING TYPES

WEATHER STATION SHIPS

TRAINING SHIPS

LIGHTHOUSE TENDERS

LIGHTSHIPS

CABLE SHIPS

WORKSHOPS

FREIGHT SHIPS

FIREBOATS

MISCELLANEOUS SMALL CRAFT

The Coast Guard now combines Navy functions with the duties it maintained in peacetime under the Treasury Department. Law enforcement, fishery protection, life-saving, and surf patrol have been discontinued, while iceberg patrol and the tending of lighthouses and other navigation aids have taken on even greater significance with wartime conditions. To these regular peacetime duties have been added an intensive anti-submarine patrol, convoy escort work, and the manning of landing craft and naval vessels.

Expanding its forces, the Coast Guard is now building long-range, well-armed icebreakers as well as acquiring fishing boats and yachts for patrol. The Coast Guard Reserve is another phase of this expansion, using small private yachts for coastal and harbor patrol.

Because of this large conversion and reserve program, it is possible to illustrate only typical boats among the smaller cutter groups. They are not indicative of the many types manned by Coast Guard personnel, which may be found in other sections of ONI 54.

Design adapted from Navy PG (ERIE Class).   Peacetime duties and appearance were similar.

CAMPBELL-7/30/43

TAMPA Class—240'

Completed in 1921. Similar to "LAKE" type cutters transferred to Great Britain: (LULWORTH Class).

▼

▼ TAMPA-5/29/42   ▲ MODOC   ▼ HAIDA-2/24/43

"A" (ESCANABA) Class—165'

Designed to serve as miniature gunboats, this class is the heavier 165' cutter type. They were used as ice-breakers on the Great Lakes.

▲ COMANCHE   ▼ ONONDAGA—4/27/43 ▼

"B" (ARGO) Class—165'

One unit serves as Presidential yacht POTOMAC. Formerly both one and two stackers, now all appear as shown.

▲ PANDORA–8/28/42   ▼ ATALANTA–12/18/42 ▼

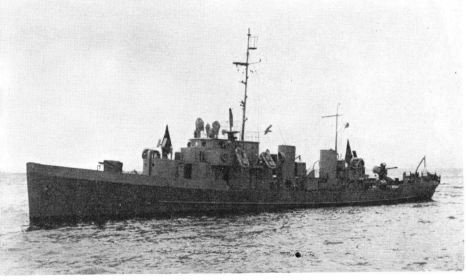

ACTIVE Class—125'

Formerly based on Great Lakes and all U. S. outposts. Now serve on convoy and patrol duty as the Coast Guard equivalent to the Navy SC.

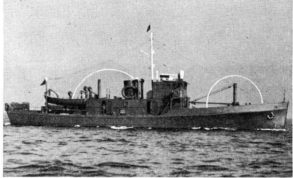

CRAWFORD ▲ Two units showing prewar rig ▲ ACTIVE   ▼ YEATON—8/6/4   ▲▼ FAUNCE—5/11/43

▲ STORIS—10/24/42   ▼ WOODBINE as Buoy Tender—6/5/43   CLOVER ▶

Based on the larger Storis (180') design and built especially for icebreaking. Have been improved in two successive classes, the IRONWOOD and IRIS type.

MISCELLANEOUS CUTTERS

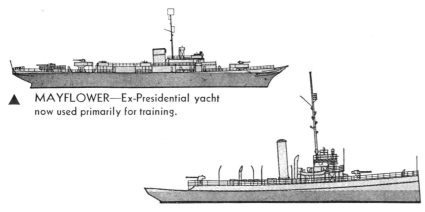

▲ MAYFLOWER—Ex-Presidential yacht now used primarily for training.

▼ GRESHAM and UNALGA, ▲ 1912 cutters modernized for patrol and escort duty.

▲▼ COBB—Ex-passenger vessel converted to floating base for helicopters in convoy wo

NORTHLAND ▲ Now used for Arctic patrol duty—7/11/42 ▲ NORTH STAR ▼ MARITA—Ex-British PG now used for training—4/26/43

▲ MENEMSHA Class—1918 "LAKE" type—7/22/43

MISCELLANEOUS SMALL CUTTERS Converted for use in coastal patrol and mine-sweeping duties.

MENHADEN FISHERMEN ▼ ROWE

WHALE-KILLER BOATS ▲ ABERDEEN–3/10/43 ▼ CADDO   TRAWLERS ▼ NATSEK–6/25/42   Navy Sisterships serve as AM, YP

TUGS—Owned and requisitioned by the Coast Guard ▼ MANITOU is typical—3/30/43.

MISTLETOE ▼ LIGHTHOUSE TENDERS—Built for the purpose or converted from various types, of which these are typical examples ▼ HICKORY—1/20/43

SUB BUSTERS

Coastal patrol craft, comparable in appearance to the Navy SC's. The 83' type is an improved counterpart of the 75' class, built during the last war. Due to their low silhouette and slight wake, these craft are often mistaken for submarines.

83' TYPE

75' TYPE

CG-74345